Equality

Key Concepts in Political Science
GENERAL EDITOR: Leonard Schapiro
EXECUTIVE EDITOR: Peter Calvert

Other titles in the same series include:

ALREADY PUBLISHED

Martin Albrow	**Bureaucracy**
A. H. Birch	**Representation**
Brian Chapman	**Police State**
Peter Calvert	**Revolution**
Ioan Davies	**Social Mobility and Political Change**
Joseph Frankel	**National Interest**
P. H. Partridge	**Consent and Consensus**
John Plamenatz	**Ideology**
Paul Wilkinson	**Social Movement**

IN PREPARATION

Shlomo Avineri	**Utopianism**
Karl Deutsch	**Legitimacy**
S. E. Finer	**Dictatorship**
C. J. Friedrich	**Tradition and Authority**
Geoffrey Goodwin	**International Society**
Julius Gould	**Violence**
E. Kamenka and Alice Erh-Soon Tay	**Law**
J. F. Lively	**Democracy**
Robert Orr	**Liberty**
Leonard Schapiro	**Totalitarianism**
Henry Tudor	**Political Myth**

Equality

John Rees
University College of Swansea

Macmillan

First published by Pall Mall Press Ltd, 1971

Published in the United States of America in 1971
by Praeger Publishers Inc.

This edition published in 1972 by
THE MACMILLAN PRESS LTD
London and Basingstoke
Associated companies in New York Toronto
Dublin Melbourne Johannesburg and Madras

SBN 333 12002 7 (paper cover)

Set by Gloucester Typesetting Co. Ltd
Gloucester

Printed in Great Britain by
The Pitman Press, Bath

Contents

'Key Concepts'
an Introductory Note

Political concepts are part of our daily speech—we abuse 'bureaucracy' and praise 'democracy', welcome or recoil from 'revolution'. Emotive words such as 'equality', 'dictatorship', 'élite' or even 'power' can often, by the very passions which they raise, obscure a proper understanding of the sense in which they are, or should be, or should not be, or have been used. Confucius regarded the 'rectification of names' as the first task of government. 'If names are not correct, language will not be in accordance with the truth of things', and this in time would lead to the end of justice, to anarchy and to war. One could with some truth point out that the attempts hitherto by governments to enforce their own quaint meanings on words have not been conspicuous for their success in the advancement of justice. 'Rectification of names' there must certainly be: but most of us would prefer such rectification to take place in the free debate of the university, in the competitive arena of the pages of the book or journal.

Analysis of commonly used political terms, their reassessment or their 'rectification', is, of course, normal activity in the political science departments of our universities. The idea of this series was indeed born in the course of discussion between a few university teachers of political science, of whom Professor S. E. Finer of Manchester University was one. It occurred to us that a series of short books discussing the 'Key Concepts' in political science would serve two purposes. In universities these books could provide the kind of brief political texts which might be of assistance to students in gaining a fuller understanding of the terms which they were constantly using. But we also hoped that outside the universities there exists a reading public which has the time, the curiosity and the inclination to pause to reflect on some of those words and ideas which are so often taken for granted. Perhaps even 'that insidious and crafty animal', as Adam Smith described the politican and statesman, will occasionally derive some pleasure or even profit from that more leisurely analysis which academic study can afford, and which a busy life in the practice of politics often denies.

It has been very far from the minds of those who have been concerned in planning and bringing into being the 'Key Concepts' series to try and impose (as if that were possible!) any uniform pattern on the authors

7

who have contributed, or will contribute, to it. I, for one, hope that each author will, in his own individual manner, seek and find the best way of helping us to a fuller understanding of the concept which he has chosen to analyse. But whatever form the individual exposition may take, there are, I believe, three aspects of illumination which we can confidently expect from each volume in this series. First, we can look for some examination of the history of the concept, and of its evolution against a changing social and political background. I believe, as many do who are concerned with the study of political science, that it is primarily in history that the explanation must be sought for many of the perplexing problems of political analysis and judgement which beset us today. Second, there is the semantic aspect. To look in depth at a 'key concept' necessarily entails a study of the name which attached itself to it; of the different ways in which, and the different purposes for which, the name was used; of the way in which in the course of history the same name was applied to several concepts, or several names were applied to one and the same concept; and, indeed, of the changes which the same concept, or what appears to be the same concept, has undergone in the course of time. This analysis will usually require a searching examination of the relevant literature in order to assess the present stage of scholarship in each particular field. And thirdly, I hope that the reader of each volume in this series will be able to decide for himself what the proper and valid use should be of a familiar term in politics, and will gain, as it were, from each volume a sharper and better-tempered tool for political analysis.

There are many today who would disagree with Bismarck's view that politics can never be an exact science. I express no opinion on this much debated question. But all of us who are students of politics—and our numbers both inside and outside the universities continue to grow —will be the better for knowing what precisely we mean when we use a common political term.

London School of Economics   Leonard Schapiro
and Political Science   General Editor

Acknowledgements

It is often difficult to identify the sources of one's ideas but my main conscious debt in working on this short book has been to the late R. H. Tawney who, through his writings and as teacher, stimulated an abiding interest in equality. His compassion and humanity were coupled with a firm grasp of the limits of political action and have always been for me an inspiring example of how scholarship can be related to social problems without loss of academic integrity.

The Warden and Fellows of All Souls enabled me to do much of the preparatory work on this volume in ideal conditions when they kindly received me as one of their Visiting Fellows. For their hospitality I am truly grateful.

I am further indebted to Mrs. Beryl Langford for typing the manuscript; to Bernard G. Mullins for many useful editorial suggestions; and not least to my wife, Betty, who prepared the index and has always provided that vital background of sympathetic interest in my academic work.

The publishers and I would further like to thank George Allen & Unwin Ltd. for permission to quote from R. H. Tawney's *Equality*.

John Rees   July 1971

1/Introductory

How is the concept of equality related to other concepts used by students of politics? At first sight there would seem to be a case for thinking that equality is not so basic and central a concept as, say, power or authority: it could be argued that the latter are essential concepts for the study of political life at any time or in any place, whereas the notion of equality has only a limited relevance. Equality, it might be said, is an ideal or principle; something men aim at or by reference to which they guide their conduct. Power and authority, on the other hand, correspond to certain enduring features of human relationships, especially when men live under government or in states. Equality is characteristically a 'reforming' idea and since the periods in human history when the zeal for improvement in an egalitarian direction constitute a fraction of man's total political experience the idea has only an intermittent importance.

Now even if this were all true, standing no need of elaboration or qualification, it would also be true that the idea of equality, in one form or another, has in modern times, especially since the seventeenth century, assumed a continuing and major role in both the theory and practice of politics. And this would be reason enough for according it a central place among the concepts of political science. But of course the idea was not born in the seventeenth century, nor has its importance in political activity or its role in political institutions been confined to modern times. A cursory study of Greek political life and thought in the classical age is enough to show that much of what enters into quite recent discussions about equality had its origins in that era.

We should not, however, assume that the concept of equality is relevant only for the study of societies in which men aspire to greater equality or in which the idea plays an important normative role in their institutions and practices; as when there is an endeavour to reduce inequalities of wealth and to secure greater equality of opportunity in education or when a society sets store by equality of voting power and equality of treatment before the courts. For certainly to think of equality exclusively in this way, that is, as either an ideal or a principle, is to put it into a different category from such notions as power and authority.

We may also be concerned with equality in a somewhat different sense—a sense that brings it closer in type to concepts such as power and authority—when we focus our attention on the ways that wealth, power, rights, and opportunities are distributed among the members of a society. And whether or not a society is highly stratified, manifests great inequalities of condition, is a matter of interest not only to the sociologist and social historian but also to the political scientist. Enquiry into the 'social structure' or the 'social system', long commonly regarded as essential for understanding the 'political system', assigns high importance to such notions as class, status group and élite. Categories of this sort imply that various social groups are differently situated in respect of power, wealth, and prestige; that they are *unequal*. The significance attributed to these inequalities in accounts of the nature of society and in theories of social change has of course greatly varied, but recognition of their importance is a common feature in the writings of the great political thinkers from Plato and Aristotle down to Rousseau and Marx, and occupies a central place in modern sociology. 'The division of society into classes or strata, which are ranged in a hierarchy of wealth, prestige, and power is a prominent and almost universal feature of social structure which has always attracted the attention of social theorists and philosophers,' says T. B. Bottomore. And, he adds, for the greater part of their history 'this inequality among men has been generally accepted as an unalterable fact'.[1] It is when men, or some of them, see certain of these inequalities as unjust and alterable that equality as an ideal becomes a potent force in political life.

Before an inequality can become the object of criticism and regarded as unjust it would seem to be a necessary condition that it should be alterable. And this is generally so, though occasionally one hears, or reads, of people who complain that nature is unjust in imposing the burden of child-bearing on women, in conferring beauty on some and inflicting ugliness on others. But by no means all alterable inequalities are thought to be unjust for, making due allowance for the variety of standpoints as to what constitutes an injustice, there are some inequalities which are accepted as socially useful, not to say beneficial. The leader of a research team in a physics laboratory would not commonly be thought to be an oppressor, exercising illegitimate or unjust power over the members of his team, any more than a doctor over his patient. It would indeed be an extreme and rare position that would hold *any* kind of relationship between men involving power, authority, or prestige to be unjust and unnecessary. Even the extreme anarchist who claims to be 'against all authority' is likely to equivocate when confronted with such facts as that a man's good works and admired achievements can lead, via the esteem and regard he gains in the eyes of his fellows, to a position of authority among them. Would he want to argue that the sort of influence Socrates exerted over his friends is an unnecessary evil?

However, the relationship between inequality and injustice and the extent to which inequalities must be alterable before they can be sensibly regarded as unjust is more complex than I have so far allowed. The Marxist position is instructive here. No one has done more to highlight the inequalities in man's condition than Marx and Engels. The categories of master and slave, lord and serf, bourgeois and proletarian stand for what they claimed were the major social divisions in human history. Despite all the talk about Marx having created a *science* of society, there can be no doubt that both he and Engels condemned the exploitation and oppression associated with these class divisions as unjust even though, from the Marxist standpoint, these divisions were *historically necessary*, i.e. *unalterable*. They were, however, unalterable only so long as the class relationships in question corresponded to, were compatible with, the productive forces at society's disposal. Eventually, of course, they would become alterable; and it was man's destiny to end all class divisions. The inequalities arising out of class societies were, therefore, alterable; but not in the simple way that a wealth tax or the abolition of public schools might alter the inequalities (or some of them) in British society today.

It is, incidentally, an error one still commonly meets with to suppose that even as regards 'the long run' Marxism adopted an extreme egalitarian position. The 'Manifesto of the Equals' might declare: 'Let there be no longer any other differences in mankind than those of age and sex'[2], but Engels is far more cautious. On the one hand he is confident that when the victorious proletariat has socialized the productive forces the role of the state in social life will become increasingly superfluous since economic production will be organized 'on the basis of a free and *equal* association of the producers'. Yet he insists that when the workers demand equality what they are really demanding is the abolition of classes: 'any demand for equality that goes beyond that, of necessity passes into absurdity'.[3] For Engels goes on to explain that although the proletariat will put an end to the state 'as the state', will abolish 'the government of persons', it will still be necessary to 'administer things' and direct the processes of production; thus giving a clear answer to the question he once explicitly raised in an essay directed at the anarchists—'is it possible to have organization without authority?'[4]

The inequalities which have struck men as unjust and stirred them to protest are of course the differences in political and social status, in the distribution of wealth and the opportunities for self-development, rather than the differences between persons in ability, personality, or esteem. How far the latter are themselves attributable to the 'social environment' and can be made to disappear in a just social order is one of the long-argued questions about equality. On the whole Engels, like most other socialist writers, seems to have shared the optimism of Robert Owen in thinking that society rather than nature makes men unequal. Yet, as he maintained against the anarchists, given the nature of modern society there must be authority, and, although he did not express himself in precisely these terms, that means inequality. If therefore the needs of an industrial economy, quite independently of the class system, demand relationships of authority and subordination, can we say that these relationships are alterable? And if we are to regard them as 'conventional' (hence alterable?) as opposed to 'natural', what meaning can the idea of natural equality have in a world of this kind? These are important issues which should be looked at more closely before we go on to sort out just what are the significant kinds of inequality and what meaning the demand for equality can have in the world today.

The distinction between what is 'natural' and what is 'conventional' appears frequently in the history of political and social thought. At the very beginning of the Western tradition of political theory it appears in those dialogues of Plato where the views of the Sophists are stated and criticized. In the first book of the *Republic* Glaucon expounds what he claimed was commonly thought about the nature and origin of justice, namely, that 'by nature . . . to do injustice is good, to suffer it evil, but there is more evil in suffering injustice than there is good in inflicting it'; so men come to see the sense of establishing 'laws and covenants' which restrict the doing of injustice. Hence justice is established by convention.[5]

In the *Gorgias* the standards established by convention are dismissed with emphatic scorn by Callicles in favour of following the dictates of nature. It is convention, he argues, that establishes equality of status because the majority, who are individually weak, are frightened of suffering injustice at the hands of the strong. Inequality is thus sanctioned by nature, and equality can only be founded on the rules and standards that men themselves make—a view which seems to run counter to what in modern times has been the more popular belief, namely, that by nature all men are equal. In the state of nature, says Locke, men are free to do as they wish and are also in a state of equality, 'wherein all the power and jurisdiction is reciprocal, no one having more than another'.[6]

Perhaps the most famous assertion about equality which makes use of the nature/convention distinction is the oft-quoted passage in Rousseau's *Discourse on Inequality*:

> I conceive of two sorts of inequality in the human species: one, which I call natural or physical, because it is established by nature and consists in the difference of ages, health, bodily strengths, and qualities of mind or soul; the other, which may be called moral or political inequality, because it depends upon a sort of convention and is established, or at least authorized, by the consent of men. The latter consists in the different privileges that some men enjoy to the prejudice of others, such as to be richer, more honoured, more powerful than they, or even to make themselves obeyed by them.[7]

The sheer persistence of the nature/convention dichotomy over the centuries may of itself seem sufficient to establish its credentials. A modern writer on equality, John Wilson, has remarked that the distinction 'is and always has been crucial for all egalitarian thinkers', yet he feels that it is beset with many difficult problems.[8] If this were to be made as a general point I would very much agree with his verdict, but when it comes to specifying the difficulties involved in drawing the distinction I have reservations about some of the criticisms he makes. But more of this presently.

Rousseau talks about differences in the 'qualities of mind or soul' (des qualités de l'esprit ou de l'âme) being 'established by nature'. In the next paragraph he mentions 'wisdom' and 'virtue' (la sagesse, la vertu) in such a way as to suggest that they are examples of the qualities he has in mind. Now is Rousseau trying to say that wisdom and virtue owe nothing to the process of social conditioning, that a man can be wise and virtuous outside society? Or is it that a man cannot be wise and virtuous outside society but that his wisdom and virtue owe nothing to society, in the way that the colour of the hair a man is born with owes nothing to society? These and other questions of a similar kind are not just the product of a fussy pedantry: they go to the heart of the problem of what it is for something to exist 'by nature' as opposed to 'convention'. It has long been a common objection to the kind of view Rousseau seems to be expounding that the 'qualities' attributed to natural man are characteristic of men living in societies, i.e. men whose relationships are governed by conventions.[9] Indeed Rousseau himself made precisely this sort of point, so much so that his initial distinction stands in obvious need of clarification. Referring to those philosophers who have felt it necessary to go back to 'the state of nature', he remarks that they attribute to natural man characteristics such as avarice and pride, thus importing into the state of nature 'ideas they had acquired in society: they spoke about savage man and they described civil man'.[10]

One difficulty in attempting to sort out the implications of the nature/ convention distinction is to discover just what the various writers who make use of the distinction mean by 'nature' and 'natural'. Are they, for example, talking about 'natural man' in the sense of a creature with human appearance who lived *before* there was human society or of a being who lives 'outside society'; or are they referring to what remains constant in human behaviour despite changing and diverse social conventions? It seems unlikely that they are all united by an agreed and carefully thought out understanding of the contrast between nature and convention or by a common definition of natural man, though A. MacIntyre claims that the Sophists' idea of natural man 'has a long history in European ethics in front of him'; arguing that despite variation of detail in the accounts given of natural man's make-up, the concept has as its core the belief that 'social life is perhaps chronologically and certainly logically secondary to a form of unconstrained non-social human life in which what men do is a matter of their individual natural psychology'.[11]

Now if this is the common assumption behind all talk of natural man and constitutes the underlying idea of the nature/convention distinction then it is of course open to powerful objection, as indeed I have already suggested. For if we set out to describe the life of 'men' in such a condition it is important, as Rousseau remarked, to rule out from the description of that life concepts and terms which get their meaning and significance from human social life. Or, as MacIntyre puts it, the terms which we use to describe the behaviour of pre-social man do in fact belong to a language which 'presupposes an established web of social and moral relationships' and for this reason the whole idea of natural man is caught up in a 'fatal internal incoherence'.[12]

The reader might feel at this stage that Rousseau's distinction between natural and conventional inequalities is not affected by general criticisms of the idea of natural man and that there could well be an element of truth in what he is trying to say. Or, at least, that if his distinction is unsound it must be shown to be so by arguments different from those so far used.

The respects in which men can be equal or unequal are, according to Rousseau, classifiable into two broad categories: (a) 'natural or physical', such as differences in age, health, bodily strength and 'qualities of mind or soul'; and (b) 'moral or political', depending upon 'a sort of convention', and including differentiations in wealth, esteem, and power.

What is it that distinguishes these two categories? At first one is tempted to say that what is natural is just there, or happens, independently of human wishes, like the Eiger or the North Pole, the weather or the growth of plants before men began to cultivate them. These things and processes owe nothing to human intervention: their existence and nature are not in any way determined by the diverse sets of norms and standards in the various human societies. The process of birth, growth, maturity, old age, and death in animal life would seem to fit into this scheme, although an animal's death can result from non-natural causes.[13] But age, at any rate, is quite outside our control and no matter what medicine may do to postpone death the difference between the old and the young, Rousseau was entitled to think, is a fact of life we cannot alter: it is something we just have to accept. Even so, the concept of age, the way we measure it and the criteria we use for distinguishing the old from the young, are not independent of human convention. Moreover some men retain agility of mind and body, partly through their own efforts, when others sink into decline. Nevertheless, despite these qualifications, let us concede that Rousseau was justified in thinking that the biological processes we call 'growing' and 'ageing' are natural in the sense described and that they result in important differences between men.

With regard to health and strength there are also qualifications to be made. Being or becoming strong and healthy is certainly not completely beyond our control. Men born weaklings (destined by nature to be weak?) have become strong and healthy by appropriate exercise and nutrition. But it is the 'qualities of mind and soul' which seem to fit so uneasily into this category. And one of the best short statements of the reasons for thinking so is provided by Rousseau himself later on in the *Discourse*. Some of the differences between men which are regarded as natural, he says, are really 'the work of habit and the various types of life men adopt in society'. He goes on:

> Thus a robust or delicate temperament, and the strength or weakness that depend on it, often come more from the harsh or effeminate way in which one has been raised than from the primitive constitution of bodies. The same is true of strength of mind; and not only does education establish a difference between cultivated minds and those which are not, but it augments the difference among the former in proportion to their culture . . .[14]

In Rousseau's second category there are the inequalities that go with some men having riches, honour or power. It is obvious why such differences should be accounted conventional rather than natural. A man's wealth cannot be separated from the laws of property and the economic system prevailing in the society. Similarly one cannot conceive of someone being esteemed or honoured apart from the standards and values of the society concerned. Now it might be on account of certain 'qualities of mind and soul' that a man is admired or esteemed; but do all such qualities elicit the same response in every known society? Just as it is not 'natural' for man to admire the conspicuous consumption of a film star or an industrial tycoon rather than the austerity of a monk, so there is no reason to suppose that wisdom and calm deliberation are always rated above demogogy and impetuosity. And from the fact that certain qualities are admired it seems reasonable to infer that society has devised ways, formal and informal, of fostering them among its members, as indeed Rousseau himself implies.

I am not arguing that we should exclude 'nature' from any part whatsoever in producing 'qualities of mind and soul', for it would be rash to assert that the difference between, say, the calm and the impetuous person is attributable entirely to upbringing and education. The point is rather that some of the qualities Rousseau seems to regard as natural (his account of what constitutes this class is not as clear as it might have been) are inconceivable outside the framework of social relationship with established rules and standards; and that some of the qualities he mentions are no less dependent on these rules and standards than 'honour' and 'power', both of which are specifically included among things conventional. We have noted that 'wisdom' and 'virtue' are given as examples of 'qualities of mind or soul'. Now the concept of virtue is surely inseparable from the idea of conforming to certain standards of behaviour and these standards are, as Rousseau seems to use the terms, a matter of convention. It might, however, be argued that we ought not to draw the line between nature and convention in this manner and that it was not Rousseau's intention to distinguish them thus. But if we are to put the character of the distinction itself under discussion this is bound to have repercussions on the assumption that we should approach the problem of equality with this very distinction as one of our principal guidelines.

How then should we draw the distinction between nature and convention: is it of any significance for the problem of equality where we draw the line? Reference was made earlier to the assertion in John

Wilson's book, *Equality*, that the distinction between natural and conventional inequalities 'is and always has been crucial for all egalitarian
thinkers'. Wilson recognizes, of course, that there are difficulties about
what is to be counted 'natural' as opposed to 'conventional' ('artificial'
is his term) and says that the distinction commonly made between the
two terms 'is actually no more than a mask that covers many different
distinctions and many difficult problems'.[15]

He develops his argument from the way the *Oxford English Dictionary*
differentiates between two sorts of equality. In the first place 'equal'
can mean identity in amount or size; and, secondly, being 'on the same
level in dignity, power, excellence . . . having the same rights or privileges'. Hence there are two kinds of equality. First, natural equality, as
when two men are of equal height or two stones of equal weight. These
are, says Wilson, facts to be noted, for the equality or identity we find
is independent of our choice or desires. And, second, artificial or man-
made equality, as when two objects are taken to be of equal value or 'two
men may have an equal voice in the government of a country'.[16] The
equality in this type of case derives from our deciding to 'count them'
as equal; that is, there could be no equality in this sense apart from the
standards of value applied, apart from the decision to *treat* them as equal.
Wilson claims that the reason why the distinction between these two
sorts of equality is important for all egalitarian thinkers is that the case
for *treating* all men as equal has been commonly based on their *being*
equal; that is, natural equality has been thought to justify equality of
treatment.[17]

The difference between the natural and the conventional, according
to this interpretation, turns on our being able to maintain the distinction
between what Wilson terms 'natural fact' (that which is given, what is
there to be noted, independent of human choice or decision) and 'status'
(things or persons share the same status or value by virtue of artificial
human standards). But, as Wilson readily points out, the attempt to
maintain the distinction has to meet a serious difficulty. Natural facts
yield equality only through the use of criteria for establishing what is
identical, similar or 'the same' and these criteria are part of an artificial
product, human language. So the difference cannot be simply described
as one between what is naturally given and what is man-made.

Wilson suggests, however, that the criteria we use are not merely a
matter of arbitrary decision; they come to be adopted because of certain
biological and psychological factors common to all men, such as the
nature and mode of operation of our sense organs. It is through observation (i.e. via our sense organs) and the use of certain commonly accepted

criteria of measurement that we determine whether things are of the same height or size, whereas questions about equality of status involve appeal to standards of a different sort; special sets of rules which, as Wilson sees it, 'are not just rules of language' but rather 'the rules of a particular game'.

He gives the example of determining the size of a hole, which involves no more than observation and knowledge of some common standards of measurement, as opposed to deciding, in chess, whether the bishop is a more powerful piece than the knight. A hole is something we find in nature; not so a chess-piece. The value or power of a piece in chess cannot be separated from the rules of a particular game and these rules are entirely a matter of human contrivance. Knowing these rules is a necessary condition of making any significant judgement about the relative power of the pieces in the game. So Wilson is led to conclude that 'natural equality consists in similarities that can be verified by observation within the framework of a language . . . whereas artificial equality of status, depends on some further set of rules, which have to be learnt if the similarities are to be understood'.[18]

The reservations I have about this account of the difference between natural and conventional (or artificial) inequalities turn to some extent, but not entirely, on the degree of emphasis Wilson gives to the various components in his argument, for the way he presents it seems to me to prevent what is really important from getting due recognition.

Let us proceed by one or two examples. If we wish to determine whether a cheetah runs faster than a gazelle we could put the matter to the test in any one of several ways. For simplicity's sake let us assume there are just two ways open to us: first, timing the two animals separately over measured distances when we can be sure they are at top speed; and, second, noticing that the cheetah always overtakes the gazelle in chase. The second method is clearly straightforward and involves only the most elementary concepts of our language and the most rudimentary powers of observation. There would be sense in saying that we are simply observing a 'natural fact', namely, that the speed at which the cheetah runs is faster than that of the gazelle. It would be natural because the relative speed of the two animals is quite independent of human influence. Indeed cheetahs probably overtook gazelles before there were any men to see them doing it.[19]

The first method, however, is a much more complicated affair than simply observing a natural fact. We should have to employ instruments and techniques of measurement and thus be familiar with the rules governing the various aspects of measuring ground distance and time. Would these be, in Wilson's phrase, 'just rules of language'? Or would they constitute 'the rules of a particular game'? In other words, by appealing to such rules would we be concerned with 'artificial' rather than 'natural' phenomena? It would surely be very odd to make the use of such rules the test of the difference between the natural and the artificial, for in the case of the cheetah and the gazelle it would be the same 'natural fact' that we would be observing whichever method we used. Determining the relative heights of, say, Mont Blanc and Monte Rosa is a far more complicated business than establishing the relative speed of animals and in this case no *direct* observation (as when we can see the cheetah overtake the gazelle) is possible. Sophisticated instruments and techniques, the employment of which requires specialized training, have to be used. In respect of learning 'special sets of rules' the comparison of the heights of the two mountains is much further removed from men's normal linguistic and conceptual equipment than comparing the rights and privileges of two persons, if indeed the latter could be said to demand any unusual knowledge at all.

The important point of difference here—a point which, although he does at times seem to recognize it, Wilson does not bring out with sufficient clarity and force—is not whether we have to invoke a 'further set of rules' (this is altogether too vague a way of putting it) but the fact that rights and privileges are dependent on man-made rules in a manner that the speed of a cheetah or the height of a mountain are not. It would make perfectly good sense to say that the cheetah was faster than the gazelle before men could possibly have known the fact, whereas it would make no sense at all to say that there were rights and privileges before there was a human society. It is a necessary condition of a person's having any kind of right that there should be in existence a system of legal rules: there can be no right to property without a law of property.[20] The cheetah's speed is not dependent on a system of rules in that way.

It might be supposed from what has so far been said that the difference between the natural and the conventional consists wholly in the fact that the former does not depend on human choice whereas the latter, being man-made, is of our choosing; and this could well seem to carry the suggestion that everything man-made, being dependent on our choice, could be altered if we so choose. In regard to equality it might be thought that natural inequalities, since they are not of our making, are therefore unalterable, whereas all conventional inequalities, having arisen from human choice, can be abolished or amended as we wish.

But natural inequalities are not all beyond remedy. Some people born with defects, for example, can be provided with artificial aids which enable them to overcome, largely or partially, their natural disadvantages; or their condition can be improved by other artificial methods, e.g. surgery. (Incidentally, would a defect of this kind be 'natural' if caused by the mother taking a certain drug?) Moreover, what we take to be alterable in these matters is not eternally fixed. Developments in science have led some to predict the distinct possibility of controlling the characteristics of our offspring. Whether or not we should welcome such power it would undoubtedly change our conceptions of what is natural and it could well be used to eliminate or, at least, reduce the inequalities in mental and physical capacity among human beings. So what depends on human choice is by no means a constant and unchanging factor, though of course at any one time there are limits which have to be accepted.

Apart from such considerations, however, the notion of choice itself seems quite inappropriate when applied to many human institutions and practices. Did the British *choose* to have an industrial revolution? If so, in what sense? Certainly not in the sense in which, say, voters in Wales can choose to have public houses open on Sundays. Given that men did not choose or decide to have modern industry and that it is now here on a large scale, are not many social developments (e.g. everything that goes with conurbations) substantially beyond our control? One does not have to go all the way with the Marxists and claim that certain social arrangements are inevitably or necessarily connected with the state of technology, yet the room for manoeuvre at any particular stage of economic development is clearly restricted. To take an extreme example, it is not open to citizens to adopt a system of nomadic tribes in Britain or the United States today. Moreover the nature of large-scale industrial enterprises and the requirements of economic efficiency would seem of themselves to make for important inequalities. Now, assuming we wish to eliminate or mitigate these inequalities, will it help to try to determine what is natural or what is conventional in this context?

But there is another and more radical approach to the question of what is open to men to choose in the way of human practices and institutions. This is the point of view which holds that some human practices are so essential to any form of social life that they should be regarded as necessary elements in the very idea of a human society. Such practices would, on this view, hardly be conventional, i.e. in the sense that we could abolish them if we choose. On the other hand the practices could be regarded as 'man-made'; though the ambiguity and vagueness attaching to that term may not allow us to arrive at any precise inference.[21]

Perhaps the earliest statement of this view is to be found in Plato's *Protagoras*. (Or, to put it more cautiously, what could be construed as an early version of the view can be found there.) In the dialogue Protagoras depicts men as needing 'the qualities of respect for others and a sense of justice' in order to survive as a species living in ordered society, 'for a man cannot be without some share in justice, or he would not be human'.[22] It would surely be an implication of what is said here that a sense of 'justice' (or 'right') involves behaving in one's dealings with others in certain ways and that this kind of behaviour is essential to the functioning of human society; and it would be a further implication that civilized human beings have no choice but to observe those practices which are consistent with this sense of right. Thus it may not be fanciful to claim that, according to Protagoras, there are some essential features of human society; that so long as we remain 'human' those features will characterize our societies. In this way it could be said that the area of choice as to what institutions and practices we have is restricted: to put it negatively, we cannot choose or decide to abolish *any* kind of human practice.

What is said in a general or even vague manner by Protagoras, leaving room for diverse interpretations I would agree, is stated with brilliant clarity and definiteness by David Hume. In the course of his celebrated account of the origin of justice and property he makes some remarks on what is natural and what is conventional in human behaviour which have much relevance for our theme. According to Hume there are three practices essential for the existence of society: the stability of possessions, the transfer of possessions by consent and the fulfilment of promises. The peace and security of society depend on the strict observance of these practices. Yet necessary though they are 'to the support of society' they are at the same time 'entirely artificial and of human invention'.[23] Thus Hume concludes that justice, which is inseparably bound up with these practices, is an artificial rather than a natural virtue. But he also describes his three basic practices as 'fundamental laws of nature'. So what are laid down as the necessary conditions of human society turn out to be both natural and conventional. And at first sight this must appear very confusing. Hume, however, points out that the idea of what is natural is not free from ambiguity. What is natural may be contrasted with what is rare or unusual, but also with what is artificial. In a passage in the *Treatise of Human Nature* he makes his position clear:

... when I deny justice to be a natural virtue, I make use of the word *natural*, only as opposed to *artificial*. In another sense of the word, as no principle of the human mind is more natural than a sense of virtue, so no virtue is more natural than justice. Mankind is an inventive species; and where an invention is obvious and absolutely necessary, it may as properly be said to be natural as anything that proceeds immediately from original principles, without the intervention of thought or reflection. Though the rules of justice be *artificial*, they are not *arbitrary*. Nor is the expression improper to call them *Laws of Nature*; if by *natural* we understand what is common to any species, or even if we confine it to mean what is inseparable from the species.[24]

If there were an abundance of the things we desire or if the generosity of men were not limited there would be no need of justice. Men's condition therefore generates the need for securing stability in their possessions, but the remedy for that condition is derived not from nature but from artifice, that is, 'by a convention entered into by all the members of the society to bestow stability on the possession of those external goods, and leave every one in the peaceable enjoyment of what he may acquire by his fortune and industry'.[25] Hume explains that by 'a convention' here he does not mean a promise made by men to each other at a certain point in time but rather something which emerges from a growing sense of mutual interest. The rules which establish stability of possession develop gradually and become effective only slowly as our frequent experiences of the inconveniences suffered from their absence bring home their necessity.

A number of modern writers argue along lines similar to Hume. Thus Professor H. L. A. Hart contends that human activity gets much of its sense from the acceptance of survival as an overriding goal, and that given this aim, together with some elementary facts about human behaviour, we can arrive at 'certain rules of conduct which any social organization must contain if it is to be viable'. These rules, says Hart, amount to 'universally recognized principles of conduct' and he proceeds to describe them as 'the *minimum content* of Natural Law'. It is interesting to note the points of resemblance between Hart and Hume (to whom he specifically refers in one passage). Limited altruism and scarce resources are two basic features of the human situation as Hart sees it and constitute two of the several factors from which he derives his 'natural laws'. Among the latter he includes rules requiring respect for property and for its transfer, and rules which 'secure the recognition of promises as a source of obligation'.[26]

Peter Winch is another contemporary writer who maintains that some practices are so central to any sort of human social life that it is absurd to think we can choose whether or not to abolish them. Furthermore he brings out forcibly the confusion implicit in the way some have tried to draw, and make use of, the distinction between nature and convention. He argues against the possibility that, because some standards of behaviour do vary widely and are subject to change within particular societies, all norms of behaviour are merely conventional and therefore alterable and are to be regarded as on a par with, say, fashions in men's hair style.

Many philosophers have contrasted the 'laws of nature', which are said to operate unvaryingly over time and place, with human standards of behaviour, which do vary and hence are thought of as norms we can choose to abolish, retain, or modify—there being, of course, no such choice open to us in regard to laws of nature. But, Winch asks, is the choice in fact a completely free and open one in the realm of social practices? Would there, for example, be any more sense in proposing the adoption of child sacrifice in our society today than in proposing the abolition of a natural law? More positively, there are some practices we would in vain seek to abolish. 'The notion of a society in which there is a language but in which truth-telling is not regarded as the norm is,' Winch contends, 'a self-contradictory one.' It would therefore be absurd to regard the norm of truth-telling as a convention, if by that we mean a practice that it is open to us simply to adopt or reject.[27]

At this stage the reader may well ask what bearing this concern with nature and convention, and with the problem of whether there are certain enduring features of human society, has on the idea of equality. Let us therefore take stock of the situation.

Human societies have for the most part been divided into classes or groups whose members have been distinguished by the possession or lack of various advantages, opportunities, rights, powers, and privileges. Most political philosophers and social theorists have recognized and attached importance to this phenomenon, both as a significant explanatory factor and as something that needs either to be accepted, and perhaps justified, or condemned and therefore changed. The extent to which these inequalities are alterable, and hence capable of being removed, has been a persistent theme in the long-standing debate on the subject, and the form in which the issue has often been explored is that turning on the conception of 'nature' versus 'convention'.[28] But we have noticed the difficulties in the way of a clear and consistent line of demarcation separating the 'natural' from the 'conventional'; and from our brief survey we emerge with no reasons for identifying the 'natural' with what is immune to change and the 'conventional' with what could be changed if we so choose. Nor would it appear that the case for *treating* men as equals because they are *naturally* equal can derive much support from the kinds of arguments so far noticed, though this is a problem to which I shall later return.

All this suggests that the questions to explore further are, (i) whether the inequalities regarded as the most significant are alterable and, if so, (ii) whether they *should* be altered. To repeat, these are not the same questions as those implied in the nature/convention distinction. And connected with these questions is the problem of whether any of the practices and institutions which are claimed to be essential features of human society are associated with the inequalities considered to be important in such a way that demands for their removal can be shown to be either realistic or utopian. For at first sight the fact that the practices of promise-keeping and truth-telling, and rules for ensuring stability of possession, are asserted to be permanent features of society does not seem to carry with it any obvious conclusions so far as the possibility of remedying inequality is concerned. Yet, as a brief consideration of one example may show, there could be connections which a mere surface inspection will not reveal.

It has been argued that every society has had, and will continue to have, a ruling élite which discharges the key functions of government. Now it belongs to the concept of a political élite that it has certain powers and privileges which mark it off from the rest of society. Clearly this, if true, would be widely regarded as a significant form of inequality. In the eyes of those who put forward this argument it is a form of inequality which we cannot alter. (The reasons they have for saying this do not concern us here and will be considered presently.) At first glance there may not appear to be any obvious and direct connection between this alleged fact about ruling élites and the claims of writers such as Hume and Hart that there are certain necessary characteristics of human society. But a little reflection points to the possibility of an indirect relationship, namely, that if rules for securing stability of possession are indeed a necessary feature of social life then there must be provision for making, amending and enforcing these rules and this implies the necessity of some kind of ruling group, if only with limited functions, with the consequent inequality which the existence of such a group surely involves. Similar considerations apply to promise-keeping in that the fulfilment of one type of promise, i.e. contracts, has for long been and seems likely to continue to be an essential condition of a commercial industrial society. Rules governing and providing for the enforcement of contracts must therefore be made and amended, all of which again points to certain limited functions of government and hence the existence of a 'ruling class'. However, the contention that the necessity for rules about property and for a generally observed norm of promise-keeping entails the existence of government, and therefore of a ruling class, has not of course gone unchallenged. It is not my intention just here to enter that controversy. My purpose is simply to suggest a way in which the claims of Hume and other writers as to certain necessary rules of human conduct might be relevant in explaining some features of social inequality.

2/Inequality of Wealth

We come now to consider some of the main sorts of inequality and the degree to which they can be altered. Bottomore observes that for most of history men have generally regarded inequalities in wealth, prestige, and power as 'an unalterable fact' and that it has only been since the eighteenth century, when the great revolutions in America and France gave stimulus to such enquiry, that serious study has been made of the phenomenon of social class 'as a stark embodiment of the principle of inequality'. Moreover it is only since the eighteenth century that these inequalities have become *widely* questioned and criticized from the standpoint of social justice.[1] Now, as we have already noted, it is not *all* inequalities which are usually questioned in this way; so it is necessary to pinpoint those inequalities that have been thought to matter, those which have come in for most criticism. Whether these are alterable is clearly an issue of great importance. As to the inequalities no one complains about, it would be interesting to determine whether this is because they are believed to be unalterable, because they are felt not to matter or because, though they *do* matter, they are regarded as beneficial in some way or other.

There may be a few who either resent or regard as unjust the fame acquired by people who stand out in various spheres of life, whether in science, the arts, politics, sport, or popular entertainment. A literal and narrow interpretation of the famous declaration in the 'Manifesto of the Equals' would seem to call for the abolition of such distinctions. 'Let there be no longer any other differences in mankind than those of age and sex,' proclaims the manifesto. Buonarroti, however, informs us that the leaders of the conspiracy were unwilling to publicize the manifesto, drawn up by Maréchal, because they disapproved of such assertions as: 'Perish the arts, if need be, provided that real equality may remain with us.' And herein lies an important aspect of the problem before us; for Maréchal's companions are likely to have concluded that given certain forms of activity, such as the arts, some men will perform with distinction, and if value is attached to the activity in question so their performances will receive recognition, though not necessarily by the formal award of honours. This of itself constitutes a source of inequality.

Accordingly we find in Buonarroti's text signs of a more cautious approach, having the primary purpose of ending the great disparities in power and wealth, as in the following passage:

> From the unequal distribution of wealth and power arise all the disorders of which nine-tenths of the inhabitants of all civilized countries justly complain. From thence result to them privations, sufferings, humiliations, and slavery. . . . It is, therefore, to restrain within just limits the *riches* and *power* of individuals, that all true social institutions should tend—power, by subjecting all citizens equally to laws emanating from the whole—and riches, by providing such institutions for distribution, as would give to each enough, and to nobody more than enough.[2]

We should notice that it is not strict equality Buonarroti is after but the restriction of wealth and power 'within just limits'; a formula as likely to attract widespread assent as to provoke highly divergent interpretations. Similarly the amount of wealth which would constitute 'enough' and the construction to be put on 'laws emanating from the whole' are far from clear. But leaving aside for the moment these and other objections which one might bring against the looseness of expression so often found in egalitarian writings, 'power' and 'wealth' are two of the most frequently cited forms of inequality which Buronarroti and other egalitarians wish either to abolish or to limit.[3]

Power and wealth, however, are not necessarily independent variables. A man's wealth can bring him power and of course power can be a means of acquiring wealth. Still, wealth could involve no more than the ability to command goods and services, just as a man of power could live and die with little wealth. Moreover both power and wealth can be connected with prestige in similar ways. But whereas wealth is a relatively simple variable to deal with, power is a very complex phenomenon.[4] A judge has power, but so also did Al Capone. And the distinction is not merely between what is or is not lawful, or legitimate, because the power of the Pope differs from that of Billy Graham and both are in a sense legitimate.

A London Sunday newspaper recently produced in weekly instalments short biographies of a thousand people who had helped to shape the twentieth century, ranging from Bix Beiderbecke and Sibelius,

Kafka and Wittgenstein to Einstein and Lenin. If influence is a form of power then they could all be said to have had power: certainly they all had prestige. To repeat, it is unlikely that many egalitarians harbour the design of eliminating, or perhaps even restricting, all forms of influence, power, and prestige; distinctions have to be drawn between what are regarded as desirable and undesirable kinds and degrees of these attributes. So the first task is to identify some of the significant forms of inequality which in our time give rise to most complaint; for whether and how to abolish or restrict them, if they can be altered, is a problem which can only arise once they have been identified.

There would be little or no dissent from the judgement that one of the outstanding facts about inequality among men is the great disparity in the ownership of wealth. At least this is true of many societies today and it was one of the features of English society which struck R. H. Tawney so forcibly when he first published his *Equality* in 1931. One of the chief characteristics of the English class structure, he wrote, 'is the division between the majority who work for wages, but who do not own or direct, and the minority who own the material apparatus of industry and determine industrial organization and policy'.[5] The figures relating to the distribution of wealth which were available for the original edition of his work suggested that in 1919 less than one per cent of the population held two-thirds 'of the aggregate wealth of the nation'.[6] In his preface to the 1938 edition he found the situation substantially unchanged;[7] and in an introduction to a later edition Professor Richard Titmuss remarked that 'still the most striking fact about British society is the great concentration in the ownership of personal net capital'.[8] The figures he quotes relate to the 1950s and show 1 per cent of the population owning 42 per cent, and 5 per cent owning 67·5 per cent, respectively, of personal net capital; figures which he claims tend to underestimate rather than exaggerate the real state of affairs.[9]

A more recent estimate is that in 1960, 5 per cent of the population owned 75 per cent of all private property in the United Kingdom, compared with 79 per cent in 1936–8.[10] Whatever the precise figures for other countries it cannot be denied that this kind of disparity is widespread; but there is also a considerable variety in the amount of inequality in the ownership of wealth between, for example, Norway and New Zealand on the one hand and Britain and West Germany on the other. Now for those who regard great disparities in the distribution of wealth as an intolerable injustice and want to embark on gradual or drastic measures for their removal or alleviation a number of remedies are available. There can be no question of this kind of inequality being unalterable.

If one's aim is to put an end to inequality in personal wealth as soon as possible, regardless of consequences, one could introduce a law or set of laws (perhaps a revolution is an indispensable preliminary to doing this) putting all land, industry, and commerce into state hands without compensation (or with as little compensation as may be necessary to avoid 'extreme hardship'), together with a capital levy on all other forms of wealth above a certain figure. Something like this was done in Russia after the Bolshevik Revolution and has since been repeated, in varying degree, in a number of other countries. Such suffering as may be involved for the rich minority was held to be massively outweighed by the benefit to the masses and the gain in social justice. But drastic procedures of this sort have little support in, for example, Britain and the consensus among those who want to move in that direction is in favour of measures such as the capital gains tax, estate duty, an annual wealth tax, and a tax on gifts 'inter vivos'.

I do not propose to go into detail on the justice or otherwise of such measures or on their social, economic, and political effects, for example, the claim that securing greater equality of wealth is a necessary, though not perhaps sufficient, means to achieving greater equality in other spheres.[11] But it should be noted that there is much less confidence nowadays in the ability to secure an immediate and substantial mitigation of mass poverty and suffering merely by a drastic redistribution of wealth.[12] This seems to be especially true of countries such as India where the problem of poverty is most acute. And in the richer societies interest in redistribution is unevenly spread as between countries as well as fluctuating in intensity over time.

When Professor J. K. Galbraith first brought out *The Affluent Society* in 1958 he declared: '. . . few things are more evident in modern social history than the decline of interest in inequality as an economic issue. This has been particularly true in the United States. And it would appear, among western countries, to be the least true of the United Kingdom . . . inequality has ceased to preoccupy men's minds.'[13] He mentioned a variety of reasons for this decline of interest and considered that they were all connected with economic growth: 'production has eliminated the more acute tensions associated with inequality . . . increasing aggregate output is an alternative to redistribution or even to the reduction of inequality'.[14] Events in the United States during the following decade, particularly the unrest among the black population, have made this appear a somewhat complacent judgement, while the widespread revival of radicalism among the young after years of either conformity or indifference has brought the question of inequality in wealth back into the arena of public debate.[15]

Inequalities in the distribution of income are perhaps not so manifestly extreme as in the distribution of wealth, at least in Britain. In countries such as India the contrast is indeed a grim and stark one: between the vast riches of the few at the top of the pyramid and the abject poverty of the millions at the bottom. For those at the bottom it is the meagre nature of their current incomes rather than lack of property which makes existence so precarious. But even among more fortunate peoples the disparities are great. According to a recent estimate the poorest one-eighth of the population in Britain receive 3·5 per cent of total personal income whereas the richest one-eighth receive ten times as much.[16] As with ownership of wealth, so with incomes there are means available for reducing these disparities, both at source, for example by state control of incomes, and by taxation.

The nature of the effects and the desirability of moving in the direction of greater equality of incomes are of course matters of controversy. Even in countries with Marxist rulers and ostensibly dedicated to the ideal of social justice, strict equality of incomes has not been a declared objective, though some, Cuba for example, appear to be more egalitarian than others, notably the Soviet Union. This is not altogether surprising, for the Marxist's emphasis on the *ownership* of wealth and his relative lack of concern with other forms of inequality derive from the central place accorded in the Marxist theory of class to the ownership of the instruments of production.[17] And herein lies an important difference in principle on the approach to the study of social inequality and the phenomenon of class in modern sociology.

I wish here to enter a reservation about the degree to which the distribution of incomes and wealth can be altered, since I could well be understood to be claiming that the question of redistribution is a simple one, merely a matter of having the desire to use well-known and tried egalitarian devices. To say that certain arrangements and practices are alterable is not to imply that we are, to use Professor Oakeshott's phrase, confronted with a blank sheet of infinite possibility. Things can be otherwise, but how long they will take to change and the extent of the change, are matters on which social science can make no sure judgement. The conventional wisdom of the historian suggests that there are ill-defined limits to the changes a society can undergo. To take an extreme case: well outside those limits would be the introduction of the Indian caste system into Britain during this century. It would, however, be to misunderstand radically the nature of the obstacles in the way of a change of this character merely to say that public opinion would be against it, for public opinion, or the bulk of it, is against many proposals which could conceivably win favour over the next three decades: for example, the abolition of the monarchy or the relaxation of the law relating to drugs. British public opinion has changed in recent years over the death penalty and homosexual conduct between consenting adults, but in both cases there had long been active minorities advocating change. More important, however, the changes were accommodated within, and were partly inspired by, existing attitudes and assumptions on a whole set of related questions. The proposal to establish a caste system in Britain would go against all the widely shared beliefs about equality which constitute a significant element in the nation's political culture. There is no foothold in British social life, in British ideas about politics and society, where a proposal of this kind could establish itself. The background of assumptions, especially the prevailing religious beliefs, which defined what was important in life, thus giving sense to the particular arrangements of the caste system as they arose, is so utterly different from the British that the proposal would, *ab initio*, sound so bizarre as simply to rule it out of serious consideration.

Now, clearly, proposals to effect substantial changes in the distribution of wealth are not of this order, but there are certainly limits to what can be achieved in the short run if one does not wish to run counter to a number of widely accepted principles of public life, principles which have a meaning both for many ardent egalitarians and upholders of the *status quo*. Short of this, however, there may be no significant interest in reducing inequalities of wealth.

At the time when he wrote *The Affluent Society* it seemed to Galbraith that public opinion in the United States had no interest in the question of equality and so the prospect of any serious movement for change in the pattern of distribution appeared quite remote. If therefore the bulk of public opinion is firmly against any radical alteration in favour of equality, no matter how unjust the existing distribution may seem to the small minority clamouring for change, to insist that present inequalities are in principle alterable is to leave out of the situation a crucial factor: namely, whether there is a desire for change. It is true that in some societies rulers of the Stalin or Mao type have embarked on large-scale upheavals in the pursuit of certain goals with little public support apart from control of the organs of coercion and such enthusiasm as can be conjured up by the monopolistic use of the mass media, but the context I have primarily in mind is that of the liberal-democratic state, where standards of public life impose a restraining influence on legislative proposals and where there is a commitment to gradual rather than violent change. In this context the idea that the room for social change, and in particular for egalitarian measures, is anything like unrestricted is plainly false.

Some indication of the sorts of restraints I am referring to is to be found in a well-known paper on 'Equality' by Roy Jenkins, written for the *New Fabian Essays* which appeared in 1952. Jenkins declared himself an egalitarian and claims to be more so than the Marxist-Leninists whom he accuses of being 'more interested in capitalist maldistribution as a flaw to be used for the overthrow of the system than as an evil to be rectified for its own sake'.[18] He regards the struggle for equality—a society 'in which men will be separated from each other less sharply by variations in wealth and origin than by differences in character'—as one of the central issues in political life 'for many decades to come'.[19] The obstacles to attaining an egalitarian society, as he then foresaw, were the tendency in British history for radical reform to come in small doses and at infrequent intervals, and the increasing number of people who would become satisfied with the benefits of 'welfare capitalism'. For these reasons he had no expectation that the movement towards equality would be rapid and welcomed this prospect as clearly preferable to a social upheaval designed to achieve equality by a sudden and dramatic blow. He took the view that the change in behaviour required for the smooth working of a classless society, such as the greater role of non-monetary incentives in securing effort and skill, would be a long-term business.

Jenkins moreover insisted—and this is crucial to what I have been arguing—that 'great changes must be made within a framework of widespread consent'; both because this is in itself the right way to go about making reforms and because of the dangers to democracy from a sudden and total assault on inequalities of wealth and income.[20] Among the measures he discusses for attacking inequality are the capital levy and the extension of public ownership. On the former he pleads for moderation, suggesting that the state continue to pay some of the income out of appropriate properties to the former owners. As to public ownership, he maintains that, short of wholesale nationalization (which he does not favour), compensation must be paid to expropriated owners, otherwise particular owners would be discriminated against in contrast to those whose industries remained in private hands.

From this brief summary of Jenkins' views I feel at the very least entitled to conclude that of the main British political parties, Labour, the one which has most identified itself with removing inequalities of wealth and income, has among its more influential leaders men whose commitment to liberal-democratic methods and desire to avoid hardship to the victims of reform make it unlikely that the party will attempt a total and sudden assault on inequalities in income and wealth. Furthermore, the important question of how far income differentiation is required as a means of inducing effort and rewarding skill and responsibility shows no sign of becoming soluble by short-term and drastic political action. All of which seems to me to justify the contention that the scope for removing inequalities in wealth and income in the near future—in certain societies at least—is far from being unlimited, conceivable, and perhaps desirable, though a close to a strictly equal distribution might eventually be.[21]

We have noticed that wealth, power, and prestige are commonly singled out as the most important forms and sources of inequality. In the Marxist view wealth is taken to be the most significant fact, its distribution being itself determined by the ownership and hence control of the means of production. The main criterion of class, in this account, is the position of various groups in respect of forms of property, i.e. land, industrial capital, and labour-power.

The emphasis given to the ownership of the sources of wealth by the Marxist marks him off from other students of social inequality who, in their enquiry into what they call 'social stratification', adopt what may be termed a pluralistic model in contrast to the monocasual one attributed to Marxism. Marx and Engels, however, qualified some of their more daring generalizations (e.g. that the mode of production determines the whole social superstructure) and in respect of class some indications can be found in their writings that the ownership of the means of production was for them neither the sole, simple, and automatic criterion by which to test the existence of social class nor the sole cause generating it. Moreover, it is obvious that Marx would not have sought to explain the influence and prestige of, say, a Gandhi or an Einstein merely in terms of their relationship to the means of production. Nevertheless, the Marxist is sufficiently committed to stressing the importance of ownership in the productive instruments to regard this fact as the prime and decisive factor in generating social inequalities; hence his conviction that the social ownership and control of these instruments is the necessary and sufficient condition for achieving a classless society.

Whether or not such a society would still manifest class divisions in a sense of class used by other sociologists is, of course, a controversial question and would seem to depend, in part at least, on the criteria we adopt for determining class. But the point I want to concentrate on here is the role of the distribution of wealth in relation to some other significant forms of inequality. For there would be common ground among Marxist and non-Marxist thinkers that wealth carries with it great advantages for its owners, even if they disagree over the question of how far a society is dominated or ruled by those who control the instruments by which wealth is produced.

In some societies wealth or poverty can make the difference between being adequately fed or undernourished—or even dying of starvation. In these societies, too, clothing, housing, and education are in varying degrees related to the size of one's wealth. On the assumption that malnutrition is no longer a serious problem in advanced industrial countries —an assumption that would not go unchallenged—the disparities in housing conditions are acknowledged to be still enormous and wealth remains a significant factor in determining, among other things, the range of one's educational opportunities, job prospects and quality of medical treatment. And since education and occupation often figure among the multiple criteria of social class in much of non-Marxian sociology, wealth, either directly or indirectly, is clearly a leading factor in producing those inequalities that attract most attention from social investigators.

The egalitarian who emphasizes the maldistribution of wealth as one of the major forms and sources of inequality has therefore a great deal on his side to justify his conviction that the ideal of securing to each person the conditions necessary for the good life (what this ideal implies we shall have to take up later) is unattainable without a redistribution of wealth. This is not to say that all egalitarians think of elimination of the gross inequalities in ownership and income as of itself sufficient; but they would certainly be virtually unanimous in holding it to be necessary. Further, the general belief among egalitarians that the distribution of wealth is something we can control and modify in accordance with our aims is, subject to the reservations entered earlier, well grounded.

Yet some of the long-standing disputes in political argument centre on the consequences of attempting to reduce inequalities of wealth. Quite apart from the possible effect on incentives and the question whether it is unjust to equate rewards among persons with varying degrees of skill, talent, responsibility, and industry, there is the claim that the accumulation of wealth in private hands can be an important safeguard against excessive state power and hence a bulwark of liberty.[22]

3/Political Equality: I

It has long been a commonplace that the formal guarantee of equality of political rights can be distorted or even wholly vitiated by inequalities in the distribution of economic power. Yet upholders of democracy have generally asserted that it is a political system which, among other things, incorporates the idea of political equality. Thus in a typical short description of democracy Henry B. Mayo says: 'A democratic political system is one in which public policies are made, on a majority basis, by representatives subject to effective popular control at periodic elections which are conducted on the principle of political equality and under conditions of political freedom.'[1]

This sort of account of democracy, and the arguments adduced to support it, derive in large part from the persistent demand of egalitarians that all men should not only be provided with the bare means of existence but also with the means to live full and happy lives. And it has been taken as a corollary of this demand that all men have a right to participate in the political life of their societies; a demand commonly expressed as the right to political equality. In some of the classical writings of democracy the case for political equality is stated in what might be called both 'absolutist' and 'instrumental' terms. It is argued that each and every adult has the right to participate in political life because such participation is held to be a necessary element in his self-development. And it is further argued that the universal possession and exercise of political rights are an essential safeguard against the abuse of power or, more positively, an essential means of ensuring that rulers promote the interests of their subjects. Thus J. S. Mill in *Representative Government*:

> It is a great discouragement to an individual, and still a greater one to a class, to be left out of the constitution; to be reduced to plead from outside the door to the arbiters of their destiny, not taken into consultation within. The maximum of the invigorating effect of freedom upon the character is only obtained when the person acted on either is, or is looking forward to becoming, a citizen as fully privileged as any other. What is still more

37

important than even this matter of feeling is the practical discipline which the character obtains from the occasional demand
made upon the citizens to exercise, for a time and in their turn,
some social function. It is not sufficiently considered how little
there is in most men's ordinary life to give any largeness either
to their conceptions or to their sentiments.

And further:

. . . the rights and interests of every or any person are only
secure from being disregarded when the person interested is
able, and habitually disposed, to stand up for them [and] . . . the
general prosperity attains a greater height, and is more widely
diffused, in proportion to the amount and variety of the personal
energies enlisted in promoting it.[2]

Mill is clearly specifying as major criteria for the worth of a
constitution both that every person's 'rights and interests' should be
taken into consideration—which is what a number of writers have regarded as the essential meaning of a principle of equality—and that each
and every person should have the means 'to stand up for them'. In
terms of actual political machinery this has been held to require, at the
very least, a system of universal franchise. But, it would be widely
accepted, universal franchise, of itself, is not enough to secure political
equality. There are a number of ways in which an electoral system,
while granting the vote to everyone, can fail to assign equal voting
power to each adult citizen and within the ranks of liberal democrats
there has been a long and continuing discussion about the most effective
means of ensuring that electoral machinery is truly democratic. And as
even a brief survey of the controversy shows, political equality turns out
to be one of several competing values in democratic theory, with the
result that electoral systems in what are commonly regarded as liberal
democracies vary considerably in the extent to which they assign importance to securing equality of voting power.

However, universal franchise, insufficient though it may be, is
nevertheless a necessary condition of political equality and it is usually
defined to mean that, whether the age of adulthood is fixed at 18 or 21,
all persons reaching that age, with a few minor exceptions, are entitled
to vote, regardless of sex, occupation, race, religion, or wealth. Further,
it would now be generally contended, it means that no adult should have

more than one vote. Plural voting, whether by virtue of the possession of property or of a university degree, runs against the almost universally held principle of 'one man, one vote'. But we should remind ourselves that British electoral law has only recently accepted this principle. And, as we shall see, there are still a few voices today raised against what they regard as the unreflecting worship of mathematical equality.

Now if we assume that every adult should have one, and not more than one, vote it would seem a logical corollary of this principle that everyone's vote should have equal weight, at least if we make political equality our main aim. Yet, to use the example of British elections, a number of practices are followed which go against this aim; for example, the great variations between the sizes of the electorates in the largest and smallest of the constituencies, unfair demarcation of constituency boundaries (a charge made especially against the electoral districts in Northern Ireland which has its American equivalent in gerrymandered districts) and the simple plurality system of electing representatives to Parliament which, in the eyes of its critics, enables a party to achieve a decisive majority of seats while gaining less than half the popular vote. (A similar charge is brought against the American electoral college system under which a man may be, and has been, elected president with a minority of the popular vote.) These are all matters which have figured in the continuing discussion about the proper institutions for a democracy and they bring out the fact of conflict or tension between the different values or principles to which liberal democracy is thought to be committed. I shall deal with just one or two of these problems, mainly in order to bring out the implications of political equality and the competing considerations to which it is sometimes made to give way.

It was, for long, part of the radical democrat's programme that, along with the extension of the franchise, there should be equality as between electoral districts. Increases in the size of, and movements within, the population of Britain pointed to the need for a regular method for re-drawing constituency boundaries and various acts of Parliament have now provided for permanent machinery to carry out this task.

The creation of a boundary commission seemed to guarantee that the problem would be tackled on a continuing and equitable basis.[3] But in 1969 the Labour government introduced a bill which its critics alleged would have meant making only those constituency alterations that were likely to favour Labour at a forthcoming election. On the ground that a comprehensive revision of boundaries should be deferred until certain major changes in local government had taken place, the bill provided for changes in nearly 100 cases out of the 300 recommended by the boundary commission. This led, quite naturally, to the suspicion that the government was attempting to load the electoral dice in its favour and to charges of gerrymandering. The fact that the complaints were made at all, and were so readily taken up by wider circles of opinion than the official opposition, leading to much sensitiveness to the charges on the government's part, is evidence of the widespread commitment to the principle of equality of electoral districts. It was no part of the government's case that it rejected this principle but rather that important practical considerations—to do with the impending reorganization of local government—pointed to the desirability of delaying its implementation.

The controversy, it should be noted, was carried on within a context in which certain political principles were commonly accepted and the issues in dispute were clearly defined because there was general acceptance of at least part of what is understood by political equality. This, however, should not be taken to mean that any of the parties to the dispute would have political equality, in the sense of equal voting power, override all other factors, such as regard for local boundaries or the sparsity of population in rural areas.

That other factors do run counter to the strict requirements of political equality as defined by 'one man, one vote', emerges all too clearly from a study of the arguments for and against proportional representation, for one of the main principles asserted by advocates of proportional representation in support of their case is that each vote should have equal weight, that as electors our voting power should be equal. And often connected with this assertion is the claim that a representative assembly should mirror as exactly as possible the political allegiances of those it represents.

I do not want to take up this latter aspect of the argument at all fully, important though it would certainly be in any discussion of the role of representation in a democratic political system. However it is worth pointing out that the 'mirror' or 'microcosm' theory of representation derives its rationale in some degree from a concern for equality. For it claims that minorities should have a place in a representative assembly in proportion to their strength in the country and if the electoral system denies them such a place then there is no equality in voting power as between those who would, or do, vote for minority parties and those whose first allegiance is to one of the major parties. Hence the long-standing complaint by minority parties in Britain—particularly the Liberals—that the electoral system is unfair and undemocratic

A few figures will help to show why these minorities feel aggrieved. At the 1966 general election the Conservatives polled 41·9 per cent of the votes and obtained 253 seats in the House of Commons, Labour polled 47·9 per cent and obtained 363 seats, while the Liberals with 8·6 per cent of the vote got a mere 12 seats. Long experience of being under-represented has, of course, led to the Liberals contesting far fewer seats than the two major parties. In 1964, for example, they contested 365 seats out of 630. At that election they polled 11·2 per cent of the votes and won 9 seats. It has been estimated that had they fought every seat they would have won over 16 per cent of the total vote.[4]

With under-representation of minority parties goes another feature of the British electoral system, namely, that a party can win a decisive majority in the Commons with less than 50 per cent of the total poll.* Thus, supported by its majority, the government is able to push through legislation which can in no sense be said to have been approved by the majority of the electorate. So, quite apart from denying equality of voting power, the relative majority system as operated in Britain produces what is on the face of it the highly undemocratic result of a representative assembly composed of a majority party supported by less than half the electorate. In 1945, for example, Labour had a majority of 146 over all other parties in the Commons, having polled 47·8 per cent of the total vote; earlier, in 1924, the Conservatives had a majority in the House of 223 with 48·3 per cent of the votes.

One of the standard and basic objections to proportional representation charges it with excessive zeal for equality at the cost of other factors which are also important for a democratic system. And this sort of counter-claim is one we frequently encounter in arguments about equality. To push the demand for equality to its extreme limits, it is often said, means ignoring or neglecting other values such as liberty, stability, recognition of merit, regard for individuality or the need for incentives. In respect of proportional representation too we may prefer to put less emphasis on equality if we believe that in so doing we achieve, say, greater stability of government.

It is certainly possible to remove the inequalities of voting power and secure a fair representation of minority parties. We could, for instance, adopt the full-blooded system of proportional representation proposed by Thomas Hare and championed by J. S. Mill. Israel, for example, conducts its national elections along these lines and other varieties are

---

* Similar arguments about representation, under-representation and govern-mental and legislative compositions could be advanced about other countries. I am here using Britain as an example.

commonly employed in different parts of the world. But the fear in Britain is that much of what is valued in the British political system would be threatened by an exclusive regard for equality.

The details of the controversy need not concern us here, but among the major considerations making for distrust of proportional representation is the advantage—though some might see it as a disadvantage—of having a government able to carry out a coherent programme submitted to the electorate as opposed to the instability and ineffectiveness of a coalition government composed of two or more parties. Single party government, it is claimed, makes for clear, decisive, and consistent policy making, or is at least one of its necessary conditions; and this, it is said, provides the electors with a definite choice. Coalition government, on the other hand, is alleged to reduce the element of responsibility because the policies followed by a government of this nature cannot be attributed to any single party. However, for those to whom equality is the overriding principle the unfairness of the British electoral system is not outweighed by these supposed advantages—advantages which spokesmen of the minority parties would claim are in any case exaggerated by the beneficiaries of the present system. The question at issue has been nicely pinpointed by Frank Stacey. 'Is this state of affairs,' he asks, after enumerating the advantages commonly thought to be associated with the existing system, 'so desirable that it is worth overlooking the inequities of representation which accompany it?'[5]

It is interesting to note how, in a different political context, the principle of according each voter equal voting weight has been regarded as a threat to minority interests. In the British context, we have seen, it is contended by the spokesmen of minority parties that inequality in voting weight results in under- or non-representation of minority viewpoints and they put forward as a remedy some version or other of proportional representation. But in the United States voices have been raised against the application of strict equality to voting procedures because, it is said, unbridled egalitarianism in this sphere would fail to protect minority interests. The argument, of course, inevitably ranges over the whole question of representation in a democratic state. But the particular discussion I have in mind has been given its recent impetus by a number of Supreme Court decisions on the apportionment of electoral districts in the United States.

For example, in the case of *Wesberry v. Sanders*, decided in 1964, the court declared that congressional districts in each state should have substantially equal electorates. At the time of the decision districts varied considerably in the size of their electorates. In Texas, for instance, the largest was 950,000 and the smallest 216,000. The American Political Science Association had recommended that no constituency should vary more than 15 per cent from the average. According to this criterion only nine of the states which elected congressmen from districts (as opposed to the eight choosing their representatives at large) came up to standard. The Supreme Court decision had, therefore, important consequences and clearly stemmed from the principle of equality of voting strength. As Justice Hugo Black put it: 'As nearly as is practicable one man's vote in a Congessional election is to be worth as much as another's.'[6]

Critics of the Supreme Court judgements, though differing in the emphasis they put on the various factors which run counter to strict equality in voting strength, share common ground in rejecting what they consider to be the assumption of 'unrestricted egalitarianism' underlying the court's decisions. The Constitution guarantees to every citizen 'equal protection of the laws' and, so one critic argues, this protection has been widely thought of as being primarily afforded by universal franchise, with all that universal franchise implies by way of checks on the abuse of power.

Arguing from this premise the court has moved to the conclusion that voting equality must be laid down as an absolute standard; but, the criticism runs, protection of minority interests may not necessarily be secured by insisting on absolute equality of voting weight. In particular it is urged that lightly populated rural districts have solid grounds for apprehension 'when absolute egalitarianism is taken to the extreme of rejecting the retention of some protective balance for them anywhere in the state government'. And, as another critic has claimed:

> The question is whether these decisions, as based on the 'one-voter, one-vote' principle, imply the acceptance by the Court of an unrestricted egalitarianism which is inconsistent with the concept of democracy expressed in the Constitution of the United States. The answer is that the decisions do imply this. They imply a view of democracy in which the protection of minority and regional interest is not a central and definitive feature. Yet this is the view of democracy in the Constitution.[7]

What this very brief survey of just some aspects of the discussion brings out, I hope, is the way that the demand for equality can conflict and compete with other political principles. The balance struck between the various competing considerations in any actual system of government corresponds to and at the same time generates different concepts of democracy. Over the relative merits of these different concepts, and the different theories of representation embodied in them, there has been a long and continuing debate.

4/Political Equality: II

There is of course an influential body of opinion which regards all talk of political equality within the context of a society characterized by the gross maldistribution of wealth as merely superficial. No amount of ingenuity in the devising of electoral machinery, it would claim, can compensate for the profound inequalities which stem from and go with the minority control and ownership of society's productive instruments.

That there is an important connection between the economic structure of society and its political life was well understood by the classical Greek philosophers—and by many others since. But in modern times the way the connection is conceived and portrayed owes a great deal to the work of Marx and his followers. Aristotle's remark that 'justice is recognized universally as some sort of equality' rested on the assumption that men were in fact unequal in a number of significant respects. His defence of slavery was, in effect, a circular argument, based on the unquestionable datum of a 'natural' human inequality. What Marxists, among others, have done is to contribute to the creation of a climate of opinion which sees these inequalities as 'conventional', capable of being removed by appropriate political action; and, it is claimed, a necessary condition of removing them is to convert the main and decisive sources of wealth into social property.

In its simplest form this line of argument was expressed by Lenin when he affirmed:

> In capitalist society, providing it develops under the most favourable conditions, we have a more or less complete democracy in the democratic republic. But this democracy is always hemmed in by the narrow limits set by capitalist exploitation, and consequently always remains, in reality, a democracy for the minority, only for the propertied classes, only for the rich.[1]

And further:

> Only in communist society, when the resistance of the capitalists

has been completely crushed, when the capitalists have dis-appeared (i.e., when there is no difference between the members of society as regards their relation to the social means of produc-tion) ... Only then will there become possible and be realized a truly complete democracy ...[2]

In the phase between the abolition of capitalist economic rela-tionships and the destruction of the bourgeois state, on the one hand, and the achievement of communist society on the other, a dictatorship of the proletariat would be necessary, and in such a regime democracy would be less than 'truly complete'. But even so, 'Proletarian democracy is a million times more democratic than any bourgeois democracy; the Soviet government is a million times more democratic than the most democratic bourgeois republic.'[3]

A more academic version of this kind of thesis was propounded by Harold Laski. His analysis of the character of the modern state led him to the conclusion that 'the main index to the nature of any actual state is the system of economic class-relations which characterise it' for what the state does 'is to put coercive power at the disposal of the class which, in any given society, owns the instruments of production there'.[4] And among the implications of this for the 'equality of rights' of the members of such a society is the fact that 'wealth is a decisive factor in the power to take advantage of the opportunities the law affords its citizens to pro-tect their rights ... Broadly, there is equality before the law only when the price of admission to its opportunities can be equally paid.'[5] What Laski took to be a great failure on the part of the Labour leadership in his day was its inability to see that the state-power was not a neutral and impartial agency but a method of securing and sustaining capitalist relations of production; and, as a consequence of this inability, 'the failure to grasp the degree in which the relations of production permeate all other factors in society, religious, cultural, educational, social, and adapt them to the over-riding economic character of the system by which the nation earns its living'.[6]

This sort of critique of bourgeois democracy, carrying with it a clear repudiation of the claim that liberal democracy secures political equality, has been amplified and refined since Lenin's day, but the main line of approach draws heavily on traditional Marxist theory, especially the Leninist version thereof. In particular the emphasis recently given to the alleged corrupting effects of consumer affluence in the advanced capitalist countries has its roots in the Leninist theory of imperialism with its subsidiary contention that the profits derived from empire have contributed to the growth of a labour aristocracy whose aspirations are confined to improvements within the bourgeois order.

Common to all varieties of this critique is the general proposition that the relations of production (i.e. the basic division between owners and non-owners of the means of production) 'permeate all other factors in society', a proposition which received its classic expression in Marx's preface to his *Contribution to the Critique of Political Economy*. There Marx advanced the view, the meaning and scope of which is much disputed, that the entire system of productive relationships forms the economic structure of society and that this is 'the real basis on which legal and political superstructures arise and to which definite forms of social consciousness correspond'; that 'the mode of production of material life determines [or 'conditions'—the original is *bedingt*] the general character of social, political, and intellectual life'.[7]

Leaving aside such problems as the range of application of this theory and the question of 'transitional' stages in social development, the generally accepted inference among Marxists is that in a bourgeois or capitalist society the whole set of legal and political arrangements has impressed upon them the bourgeois character of their origin and purpose. Law is bourgeois law because the dominant form of property is private ownership of the means of production. To maintain law and order, which is the principal function of the coercive apparatus of the state, is to preserve the distribution of wealth in favour of the beneficiaries of the system. Hence the speed and vigour with which attacks on property are met by the full force of the civil and criminal law.

Perhaps not so obvious, however, is the whole ethos of the society which inculcates a general acceptance of existing norms and so puts at a disadvantage those who wish to challenge its ideas and institutions. Education, in all its forms and stages, and the mass media of communication are safely under the control of representatives of the bourgeois order and are securely geared to operating within bourgeois assumptions. In such conditions to talk of political equality as between those who seek to reject the existing order and those who function as its trustees (whether 'conservative' or 'labour') is to fall victim to a myth which itself acts to protect and perpetuate the system. Elections to a parliament or a national assembly are conducted in the main by parties whose leaderships are firmly committed to bourgeois values and the scope for calling into question what is taken to be a national consensus is severely restricted. Faced with a body of rules which manifests the values, and operates to the advantage, of the system there is no alternative, in the light of the failure of reformist methods over the last decades, but to resort to unconstitutional and violent methods of protest. In this way the inert mass of society may be shaken out of the torpor induced in it by the system and brought to see its true condition of bondage. Only by refusing to play the game in accordance with the rules laid down by the bourgeois order itself can the revolutionary begin to redress the inequality in political opportunities in favour of the oppressed majority.

How the situation is seen by many Marxist revolutionaries today has been well expressed by Herbert Marcuse, whose own personal sense of frustration at the one-sidedness of the message purveyed by the organs of publicity comes out clearly in this passage:

> Radical change without a mass base seems to be unimaginable. But the obtaining of a mass base—at least in this country—and in the foreseeable future—seems to be equally unimaginable. What are we going to do with this contradiction?
> The answer seems to be easy . . . We have to try to get this mass base. But here we meet the limits of democratic persuasion with which we are confronted . . . Because a large, perhaps a decisive part of the majority, namely the working class, is to a great extent integrated into the system; and on a rather solid material basis, and not only superficially . . . the left has no adequate access to the media of mass communication.
> Today, public opinion is made by the media of mass communication. If you cannot buy the equal and adequate time, if you cannot buy the equal and adequate space, how are you supposed to change public opinion, a public opinion made in this monopolistic way?[8]

The ideology of liberal democracy then, as it would be commonly presented, proclaims the ideals of liberty and equality. By equality is meant, among other things, the right of every adult person to participate in political life, including the right to vote. As voter every man stands on an equal footing with every other man, provided of course the electoral mechanism does not allow for serious over- or under-weighting of the vote. But, says the critic, this claim of political equality supposes that all men are equal in the means of political influence they have at their disposal, that all groups have equal opportunity of putting their respective points of view. And this, he asserts, is simply just not so. A class society such as the bourgeois order stacks the cards in favour of a privileged minority whose interests the existing institutions and pre-vailing norms protect and sustain. By its virtual monopoly of substantial wealth this minority controls the media of mass communication and no group which stands in radical opposition to the *status quo* can compete with it on equal terms. Political equality in capitalist society, howsoever 'democratic' its political arrangements, is therefore a mere formal right which the real distribution of social power effectively belies.

It would be out of place here to explore at length and in detail the arguments brought against, and the counter-arguments in defence of, this thesis. But before leaving the subject a few points must be made.

First of all, what is a commonplace historical observation, the argu-ments for and against the thesis have bulked large in political debate in this century, especially since the Bolshevik Revolution. Democratic socialists, or social democrats, who would subscribe to much of the Leninist critique of bourgeois democracy and, like Tawney, are highly sensitive to the inequalities of capitalist society, have nevertheless com-mitted themselves to the methods of liberal democracy for the attain-ment of their purposes, albeit at the cost of being branded lackeys of the bourgeoisie by the militant left. But the revolutionary Marxist can claim no historical priority nor contemporary monopoly in the critical analysis, and proposals for change, of the wealth-dominated inegalitarian society of the capitalist West.

Further, the social democrat can point to the grim experience of Com-munist rule, official revelations of which have done much to throw the Marxist camp into disarray. Indeed, the egalitarian dedicated to parlia-mentary democracy, while being far from complacent about the ade-quacy of existing political machinery for the realization of his goals, is fortified in his commitment to constitutional methods by the record of appalling injustices perpetrated by regimes which have scornfully dis-pensed with the elementary safeguards of liberty institutionalized by bourgeois democracy. It would not be too much to say that the real tragedy of the Prague spring was the brutal suppression of the first genuine attempt by Marxist rulers to combine liberty with justice. That the attempt, had it been allowed to proceed, would probably have brought the Czech Marxist closer to the Western socialist was one reason why the Soviet leaders had to bring it to an abrupt end.

Secondly, a critique of a type of regime, bourgeois democracy or any other, which bases its indictment on the failure to ensure genuine poli-tical equality or because the formal distribution of political rights is nullified by social and economic inequalities may be expected, directly or indirectly, to point to a state of affairs which does represent political equality or at least to provide some yardstick to estimate the varying degrees of political equality which different regimes manifest. But in the literature critical of bourgeois democracy it is not easy to find any reasonably clear guidance of this sort. For the most part it is simply assumed that with a successful socialist revolution property will be socialized and the economy operated for the public good, and that in a society of this nature the people will rule, that for the first time there will be genuine democracy. Perhaps this is to oversimplify, but what cannot be doubted is the massive inequality in political influence and power, in the capacity to put its case, between the leadership of the ruling parties where socialist revolutions have occurred and the rest of the community, consenting or otherwise.

If we are to formulate reasonably precise criteria for the existence of political equality we seem to have no alternative but to draw on the literature of liberal democracy and among the necessary conditions, as we have already noted, are: (i) universal adult franchise; (ii) freedom for every person to state, and agitate for, his political opinions without fear or favour; and (iii) the right to organize with others to achieve political ends or influence political conduct. What the specific demand of equality would seem to require is that anyone should be in as favourable (or unfavourable) a position as anyone else in the possession of opportunities to carry on these activities. Taken literally of course this is an impossible requirement and we shall consider later those élitist doctrines which take off from this important fact. What our critic of bourgeois democracy affirms is that a class-divided society distributes these opportunities overwhelmingly in favour of large property owners; that, among other things, the mass media of communication (particularly the press and television) are predominantly under the control of, or at the disposal of, the wealthy and their representatives.

Now it is true that freedom to publish one's opinions would be a hollow right if it were prohibitively expensive to do so and if their wealth enabled a small minority to gain a virtual monopoly over the organs of political publicity, especially the media of mass communication. But the actual conduct of political activity and political debate is nothing like so simple as is suggested by the rather crude distinction between the owners and non-owners of the means of production. For example, the relative circulation of Communist newspapers in Britain, France, and Italy is obviously not dependent on the nature and degree of ownership and control of the means of production; nor indeed is the measure of support, electorally or otherwise, which the parties publishing them enjoy. The reasons why, say, the Italian Communist Party plays a far more prominent part in the political life of its country than its counterparts in Britain or the United States clearly cannot be explained by the proposition that the ability to communicate political opinions to a mass audience is solely dependent on the ownership of wealth.

To this, of course, the rejoinder would be made that the Italian Communists have become 'respectable' and now play the same kind of rule in Italy as the Labour Party and the Social Democrats do in Britain and West Germany. All three parties are acceptable to the bourgeoisie because they no longer constitute a serious challenge to the system: they have all adopted the 'parliamentary road to socialism'. There is no threat to capitalism in giving Harold Wilson and Willy Brandt ample time on television; equally there is no danger to the bourgeois order from 'conceding' to the Italian Communists their own organs of mass publicity. Is there not, however, implicit in this type of reasoning the suggestion that political equality is genuine (in so far as it can ever be, short of the classless society) only when certain self-appointed representatives of the 'true interests' of the oppressed gain as much space and time in the organs of political discussion as the groups to whom the masses have hitherto given their support? But if one or other section of the militant left is entitled to make this claim, why not any one of the innumerable minority groups whose voices go largely unheeded by the bulk of society? If not, then we cannot but assume that the regime is being called upon to distribute rights and opportunities on the premise that there is really only one group (or set of groups) which strives for the true liberation of man.[9]

On the other hand, it would be absurd to deny that there are many factors favouring those political parties and groups which identify themselves with the *status quo*. Both the formal and informal processes of education and the predominant bias of the organs of publicity contribute enormously—but by no means exclusively—to generating an attitude of acceptance towards the main features of the social order and its political institutions. Yet it must not be assumed that there is nothing to be said in favour of that order and those institutions. As opposed to the literature of protest and revolt there is also a literature of acceptance, with varying shades in between, and it would be a mark of extreme arrogance to suppose that reason is all on one side and that the modes of public debate should be adjusted accordingly. Moreover the liberal democrat's claim that the institutions he favours at least allow protest to make its case and gain a public hearing is backed by the historical evidence of the rise of socialist and Communist parties to positions of great influence in a number of bourgeois states.

The suggestion was aired earlier on that political equality should be taken to imply, as one of its necessary conditions, equal access on the part of all groups and persons to the media of political publicity. Put in this general way it might sound an admirable principle, but a moment's thought will readily show how enormously difficult, nay impossible, it would be to carry out such a proposal, at least if it be taken in anything like its literal sense. All persons? On the assumption that every person would be free to engage in political activity, no matter what his standpoint, 'equal access' would presumably have to be interpreted to include only those with distinctive political positions. But just imagine the difficulty of drawing workable lines of distinction and the howls of protest from those who felt themselves unjustifiably excluded! Even so, equal access for everyone with a distinctive political viewpoint would probably mean, so far as television is concerned, so little time for each person as to render his appearance virtually useless—unless of course politics were to so oust other types of programme as to become hopelessly counter-productive. And how would we allocate peak viewing time, for the demands of equality must surely require that there be no unfair advantages in this respect? When cast in this form the demand for political equality has no chance at all of being taken seriously. As to the press, daily and periodical, the difficulties, although different, are nevertheless formidable.

What are the obstacles, in, for example, a country such as Britain, in the way of anyone who wishes to publish his opinions in duplicated or printed form? The laws relating to defamation, obscenity, incitement to violence and official secrets impose some restrictions but no political tendency could claim that its progress had been impeded merely by them. The cost of printing no doubt acts as a deterrent to some and in view of the burden it imposes generally there might be a case for a public subsidy both to extend the range of publications and to ease the situation of those already in circulation, many of which find themselves in tight financial circumstances. The fact of publication, however, carries no guarantee of a mass readership and the case we are considering is that of 'equality of access' to the *mass* media. Is this demand to be satisfied by a legal requirement that the mass circulation newspapers and journals give equal opportunity—in the news columns, articles and editorials—to all persons with a distinctive political standpoint?

It will no doubt be objected that I have presented the idea of 'equal access' in such a way as to render it absurd from the outset. What political equality implies, it might be said, is equality of access for all political *organizations.*

Again, at first sight, this may seem a reasonable proposal. Is it not an integral part of liberal-democratic theory that all points of view have a right to be heard? And, taken negatively, the proposal could be directed at the relative lack of time in television broadcasts accorded to the minority parties in Britain (as well as in America), over which there has been much complaint in recent years, or the disproportionate bias in favour of the Conservative Party in the British national daily press.

Let us grant for the moment that the two main parties in both Britain and America get more than their fair share in television political broadcasts and that there is a case for giving more time to, say, the British Liberals (who would in any case be entitled to more if their strength in the country were reflected in Parliament), the Welsh Nationalists, the Scottish Nationalists and the 'orthodox' Communists. But why stop there? These parties have already established their identity; large sections of the public know about them. What of the smaller groupings who have yet to make a significant impression on the mass public audience? Should they have 'equal access' too? As things stand now, time on British television (in the 'official' political broadcasts at least) seems to be allocated on the principle of 'to them that have so it shall be given', i.e. substantial representation in Parliament entitles a party to a major share—which could, no doubt, be justified by appealing to Aristotle's principle of proportionate equality. 'Equality of access', on the other hand, would mean that no distinctions should be made among the contenders, that all are to have, irrespective of their voting or parliamentary strength, the same amount of time at equally favourable or unfavourable viewing periods.

But if we now consider what elections really decide in Britain and America, namely, that the voters are being asked in effect to choose between two sets of party leaders to head the next government, has the majority no right to want to hear more about the policies and programmes of the principal contenders than about those of minor political sects? After all, part of what we understand by democracy is that on many questions the majority decides and so long as minorities have ways of publishing their views and the chance to gather support it is difficult to see why the majority would be wrong to support this way of allocating television time. Of course were it practicable a liberal democrat should welcome the establishment of several television networks over which a wide spectrum of political opinions could compete on roughly similar terms, but here again there is no guarantee that the mass audience will treat them all impartially.

It must not be thought that we have no reason but to be perfectly satisfied with the way the mass media treat political questions and, in particular, with the manner they afford opportunities for minorities to state their views. What I have tried to do is to bring out the difficulties involved in attempting to secure 'equality of access'; indeed what such a concept, literally applied, would imply. A remedy that has proved worse than the disease is to entrust the mass media entirely to state officials. Between that and our present arrangements there is room for improvement but if the choice lay exclusively with either one of these two there can be no doubt which is the lesser evil. For one important fact in favour of the present mode of operation is the historical record, namely, that former minority groups have broken into the political scene to become major contenders. The circumstances that enable them to do this, the social forces that contribute to the shifting of political allegiances in a 'free society' are an interesting study in itself, but it would be out of place to enquire into them here.

There are, however, certain features of social life as we know it which go against equality of opportunity in the propagation of opinions. The structure of beliefs and the prevailing norms and standards in a society at any given time, diverse though they may be, constitute obstacles to all possible opinions being taken seriously. There is a sense too in which the array of beliefs and concepts at the disposal of the members of a society determines the limits of intelligibility, governs what can be sensibly thought and said. But that is not what I have primarily in mind in this context. In our society today, for example, certain religious sects or 'back-to-nature' groups will have to overcome enormous obstacles if they are to secure equality in willingness to take their messages seriously, far less gain general acceptance. A political party standing for the restoration of the British Empire would generally be thought to be after the impossible, as would an anarchist group calling for the immediate abolition of all legal restraints. No one suggests that we put a ban on such opinions but their failure to make progress is almost as effectively blocked—in some ways more effectively—by informal resistance as other groups would be if outlawed by deliberate state action. Society is never equally fair to all opinions and it is not any conscious scheming on the part of the authorities that makes it so discriminatory in the way it treats them. In this manner 'the system' can often be 'unfair' to minority groups even when the law grants them all a formal right to be heard.

Liberal democrats often talk about the pluralistic nature of Western society, with its multiplicity of associations, pressure groups, regional loyalties, customs, and attitudes to life, and up to a point they are justified in doing so. Yet in spite of this diversity there are some opinions, some attitudes, some proposals that, to speak loosely, go against the tenor of the times. Some of his critics have thought that J. S. Mill created a problem for himself by showing awareness of this fact and at the same time calling for the toleration of all opinions and even for the questioning of well-established truths so that we may become better acquainted with the grounds of our beliefs. Whether Mill is open to this charge need not concern us here but the elements in his thought which have provoked it deserve some attention because they have a bearing on this question of equality of opportunity in the publication of opinions. They also relate to some of the factors which have been held to make for social stratification, especially in the eyes of those theorists who maintain that there are certain persistent features in social life which generate inequalities.[10]

One of the main branches of what Mill called 'science of social statics' was to establish the conditions of 'stable political union'. 'No numerous society,' he asserted, 'has ever been held together without laws, or usages equivalent to them; without tribunals, and an organised force of some sort to execute their decisions. There have always been public authorities whom . . . the rest of the community obeyed, or according to general opinion were bound to obey.'

Mill went on to maintain that wherever we find this fact of habitual obedience to government certain conditions are always present, the three principal of which he describes at some length. First, a system of education, carried on throughout life, which acts as a 'restraining discipline' and has the effect of training the individual to subordinate his personal impulses and aims to the ends of society. Second, and this is the condition which some of Mill's readers have been surprised to see affirmed by the author of *On Liberty*, 'the existence, in some form or other, of the feeling of allegiance, or loyalty', the essence of which is 'that there be in the constitution of the State *something* which is settled, something permanent, and not to be called in question; something which, by general agreement, has a right to be where it is, and to be secure against disturbance, whatever else may change . . . something which men agreed in holding sacred; which, wherever freedom of discussion was a recognised principle, it was of course lawful to contest in theory, but which no one could either fear or hope to see shaken in practice; which, in short (except perhaps during some temporary crisis), was in the common estimation placed beyond discussion'. And third, 'a strong and active principle of cohesion among the members of the same community or state . . . a feeling of common interest among those who live under the same government . . .'[11]

A good deal of what Mill says in this passage would be regarded as analytically true of the concept 'state'. If we are thinking of the *state*, rather than any kind of political system, then laws, courts and the power of enforcement would seem to be necessary conditions of its existence. And were there not some sort of 'restraining discipline', that is, common standards of behaviour, we would hardly say that there was a human society at all. But it would be a mistake to insist that all the features Mill mentions should be, as it were, fully operative before we can talk of political stability, and of social stability. In modern times there have been few, if any, states or societies where these conditions have been completely fulfilled. Perhaps totalitarian regimes, with methods of coercion at their disposal unimagined by Mill, come nearest—on the surface at least, and so long as they have endured—to satisfying his requirements. But apart from them (though noting the brevity of some of their lives) our world of the twentieth century, with its social turmoil and political upheavals, seems anything but stable. Even so, much of what Mill lays down as essential to stability is descriptively true of our social life.

No one would suggest that, in Britain today for example, there is unanimity about the basic operative principles of the system of government, but that there is 'general agreement' about them among the articulate members of our leading political parties is probably at least as true as it was in Mill's time. Certainly they are not placed 'beyond discussion', for in this century the clash of ideologies has produced a degree of self-consciousness about basic political beliefs which has few historical parallels. However, allowing for all this and taking into account the phenomena of protest and revolt, and the social repercussions of technological advance, we should not ignore the still massive degree of conformity characteristic of human behaviour, including political behaviour, in our fast-moving times.

I am not here thinking only of the authoritarian regimes which resort to severe legal sanctions and mass indoctrination in order to secure conformity, for in liberal-democratic states, though the established political class is committed to freedom and widely supported institutional safeguards exist to protect it, there are informal yet formidable pressures which restrict what is put on the agenda of serious public discussion. Similarly there is a powerful bias in favour of some ways rather than others of carrying on political activity. That the military, for instance, has played such a relatively subordinate political role in the making and unmaking of governments reflects a long-standing objection in the liberal-democratic public mind against government by soldiers, so much so that even in the armed forces themselves the thought of political intervention on a scale that has become fashionable in some parts of the world has found very little favour. In Britain, for example, government control of the press, the abolition of divorce, a return to former severity in criminal punishment, massive reduction in the welfare services, restoration of royal power in government, the legal enforcement of a strict sabbatarianism—these are but a few of the non-starters in the present political climate.

It is difficult to imagine a group seriously setting out to campaign for any of the above measures. It is possible that if it did the thirst for entertainment value on the mass media would ensure it a passing publicity. But the point I wish to make is that given the existing British pattern of beliefs and values—and I am not saying they are a matter of pure accident—none of these proposals, and many others it would be tedious to enumerate, would make significant headway. Compared with, say, the idea of a wealth tax, complete freedom for the theatre and cinema or a ban on private motoring in urban centres they would start off, to put it mildly, with heavy initial handicaps. To put it in general terms, respect or derision, praise or contempt, enthusiasm or cool indifference, will be accorded the actions and opinions which men perform and ventilate in public and this is one reason why there is no equality of opportunity or equality of access for all opinions. And it is difficult to foresee a time when things will be otherwise. Of course societies differ greatly in the extent to which they make life difficult or easy for the dissenter and the eccentric, but even in Mill, who pleaded so cogently for the encouragement of unpopular opinions, there was a recognition of this brute fact that our social life places some questions effectively 'beyond discussion'.[12]

It would be a perverse misunderstanding of these remarks to take them as an attempt to justify the repression of 'undesirable' opinions or to treat them as, say, failing to distinguish between, on the one hand, the Soviet public's general indifference to its government's persecution of dissident intellectuals, the Afrikaner's reaction to doctrines of racial justice or the Chinese government's refusal to allow its people to hear what can be said in defence of Liu Shao-chi and, on the other, the likely response to an advocacy of the flat-earth theory at a conference of astronomers, the reception likely to be given to the proposal that we treat mental illness as a sign of wickedness or the predisposition of most people in Britain to admire the discoverer of penicillin rather than the drug-pusher. That people should react in the kind of way in-dicated in these last three examples is so bound up with a society's having a system of beliefs and values that a literal demand for equality of esteem for all opinions must inevitably founder. It is perfectly con-sistent with this contention to plead for greater tolerance toward minority viewpoints and to urge an extension of the opportunities for them to be stated; just as there is no contradiction between recognizing the limits imposed by the laws of nature and at the same time seeking to improve the environment of man. That in these cases acceptance of what is possible should be construed as a recipe for intolerance or a plea for passivity would be equally absurd.

   We seem to have moved a long way from political equality. After all, it may be complained, the inequalities in political life which men commonly protest against have little to do with the selective reception accorded by society to the great variety of opinions which men can and do hold. More than that, such a discussion diverts attention from the great central issues of our time, such as the power of the established ruling classes to manipulate opinion and thus make a mockery of the idea that most of us are in any genuine sense free or have equality of opportunity in political life. But part of the task of political theory is to clarify concepts, to engage in analysis and make distinctions. This aspect of its work, it is true, does not immediately lend itself to the struggles of the political arena, but from the standpoint of scholarly enquiry it is surely a necessary first step to distinguish between the various factors that impede equality. Our enquiry shows that some of these factors are remediable, others not—so long, that is, as the context of beliefs and values in which we carry on our political activity remains substantially the same. So it will be helpful to conclude this chapter with a brief review, in part recapitulation, of these various obstacles to political equality.

   I shall take for granted an adult suffrage. On this assumption a rough and ready method of classifying these obstacles would be: (i) legal; (ii) financial; and (iii) social. Now there is clearly no equality to propagate opinions, a vital element in political equality, if some are prohibited by law. And the sad fact is that there is scarcely any country in the world that does not, in some degree, penalize some kinds of opinion by law. Soviet law appears to be loose and wide enough to prohibit any state-ment directed against the regime. At the other end of the scale the Race

Relations Act in Britain forbids the expression of certain sorts of opinion, as did the Smith Act a different sort in the United States.[13] To the extent that minorities, or even perhaps majorities, are prevented from expressing their views, in that degree they are at a disadvantage in relation to those who are free to do so. Among the conditions of political equality, then, is the freedom to express one's opinions, unrestricted by law.

However, as we have noted, the absence of legal restraint is no guarantee that those who want to publish their opinions will have the means to do so, far less the resources to organize for continuous political action. And among the obstacles to adequate publicity is insufficient finance. Without money the handicaps are formidable and for long-term political organization severe, maybe decisive. In a society where wealth is distributed unequally the advantages lie with the rich. But, to repeat, parties representing the under-privileged have managed to obtain the resources to build up large organizations and to engage in sustained and well-publicized political activity. Even groups with no enduring mass support have succeeded in launching campaigns which gain widespread, if passing, attention. I have touched already on the failure of such groups to acquire the space and time on the mass media to which they feel entitled.

When we turn to consider what I have called the 'social' obstacles to equality of political opportunity the apparent simplicity of the categories suggested comes under heavy strain. For what I have in mind are factors which are not at all homogeneous and are related to those already discussed in various and indeed in complex ways.

On the one hand I include the sort of factor implied in the claim that the whole structure and quality of intellectual and political life is shaped by the underlying economic system, with all that this would entail in the way of built-in advantages for the beneficiaries of the system. And, on the other, the fact I have just been discussing, namely, the discriminatory nature of the given set of beliefs and values which prevail in a society. These two factors, if we grant the truth of the former, are obviously related, but the latter would remain true no matter whether society were egalitarian or hierarchic, no matter what its economic system and even if the causal primacy attributed to economics were rejected. But I also have in mind such phenomena as racial or religious prejudice or a mood of hostility toward certain political trends so intense as to be punitive in its effects, e.g. the McCarthy period in the United States.

Now it is important to distinguish between the inequalities resulting from, say, anti-Semitism or anti-Catholicism or a mood of 'anti-red' hysteria and what follows from those attitudes and beliefs that form part of, or are closely related to, the general intellectual outlook of the time. True enough, neither set of attitudes and beliefs is eternal, at least in the sense of being a necessary part of the life of any known or imaginable society of human beings. Yet changes in the former generally occur while the framework of the latter remains substantially intact.

Part of the difference can be seen by recognizing that it would be absurd to complain that the present state of scientific knowledge makes it difficult to believe that the earth came into existence in 4004 B.C. and that consequently the public mood is one of prejudice, derision or scorn toward groups who hold this as an article of faith in a way that it would not be absurd to complain about discrimination against coloured immigrants in Great Britain and the persecution of Jews or Catholics.[14] Provided there is no persecution of religious fundamentalists, by law or opinion, what they suffer as a consequence of the general lack of sympathy for their beliefs is unavoidable. It is simply the result of a society's being committed to one rather than another set of beliefs and values.[15] And even the most devoted attachment to the classic liberal principles of liberty of expression and the free play of ideas will not suffice to ensure all possible contenders will start off with equal chances.

I must, however, once more insist, that in speaking as I just have of certain of the basic beliefs and attitudes of a society I do not mean to imply that all beliefs and attitudes are equally resistant to change, that we simply have to resign ourselves fatalistically to them. Thus while the introduction of a caste system does not arise as a possibility in contemporary Britain, public opinion on a range of social and political issues has undergone perceptible changes in recent years. Legislation dealing with abortion, capital punishment, homosexuality, and race relations has been both a product and promoter of significant shifts in public attitudes.

5/Is Political Equality Possible?

The relation between fact and value, between description and evaluation, is generally accounted one of the central problems of moral philosophy, but it also arises in important ways in political and social philosophy. A number of philosophers have asserted that an unbridgeable logical gap prevents us moving validly from 'is' to 'ought' and in discussions about equality we are often warned that no collection of alleged facts about human nature or about human capacities can yield the conclusion that equality of treatment is desirable. Similarly, if it is right to say that 'ought' implies 'can', that no judgement to the effect that a particular action 'ought' to be performed is valid unless it is possible to do it then the ideal of equality must be set against what it is possible to achieve. As James Burnham has written, 'A goal must be possible before there is any point in considering it desirable.'[1]

Burnham's remark was made in the course of a study of a group of thinkers he called 'The Machiavellians'. He went on:

> [a goal] is not possible merely because it sounds pleasant or because men want it badly. Before asking, for instance, how democracy can be made to work, we must ask whether in fact it can work, or how far it can work. In general, Machiavellians are very careful to separate scientific questions concerning the truth about society from moral disputes over what type of society is most desirable.[2]

One of Burnham's subjects is Robert Michels who, in his book on *Political Parties*, came to this conclusion:

> . . . society cannot exist without a 'dominant' or 'political' class, and . . . the ruling class, whilst its elements are subject to a frequent partial renewal, nevertheless constitutes the only factor of sufficiently durable efficacy in the history of human development. According to this view, the government . . . cannot be anything other than the organization of a minority. It is the aim

of this minority to impose upon the rest of society a 'legal order', which is the outcome of the exigencies of dominion and of the exploitation of the mass of helots effected by the ruling minority, and can never be truly representative of the majority. The majority is thus permanently incapable of self-government. Even when the discontent of the masses culminates in a successful attempt to deprive the bourgeoisie of power, this is after all, so Mosca contends, effected only in appearance; always and necessarily there springs from the masses a new organized minority which raises itself to the rank of a governing class. Thus the majority of human beings, in a condition of eternal tutelage, are predestined by tragic necessity to submit to the dominion of a small minority, and must be content to constitute the pedestal of an oligarchy.[3]

I have already referred to the view that inequality has been a universal, or near-universal, feature of human society. For some writers it is not enough just to point to the division of societies into classes or strata, ranged in a hierarchy of wealth, prestige, and power. This is so important a characteristic of human society, they assert, that it requires explanation; some theory to account for the appearance and persistence of inequality is needed. And among sociologists a number of theories compete for acceptance. Further, while there is common recognition of the phenomenon of inequality and its universality, there are divergent views about its necessity, as to whether there must always be inequality; whether, for example, Michels was right in asserting that the majority of human beings are in a condition of 'eternal tutelage', for ever 'predestined' to be 'the pedestal of an oligarchy'.[4] It may be that what Michels says is true of the past but that 'the twentieth century is unique in offering to men for the first time the opportunity and the means to fashion social life according to their desires', to create an egalitarian society.[5] If this is true then we could expect to have an explanation of why society assumed, and had to assume this character, before our era and the reasons for supposing that things could now be otherwise.

Probably the most celebrated and influential explanation of social inequality is the one offered by Marx and Engels, to which we have once more to turn. According to the Marxian theory, ever since the breakdown of primitive society there have been classes and the story of their opposition and struggle is the key to understanding human history. The theory purports to explain why there have been classes, why there will come a time when we shall be without them and why along with the disappearance of classes there will be no more need of the state. The future Communist society, it is commonly supposed, is one in which, in all significant respects, men will be equal. This is what we may call the 'mainstream version' of Marxism and it is the implications of this theory for political equality which mainly concern us here; for the Marxian claim seems to run counter to the school of élite theorists represented by Michels.

One of the principal issues in dispute between them centres on this question of political power. As Michels put it, even when the bourgeoisie has been expropriated a new organized minority will establish itself as a governing class. What has happened in the Soviet Union and in other countries where Marxists have seized power would no doubt be cited in support of Michels' prediction. So, in respect of two of the main sorts of inequality—wealth and power—one thesis is that even if wealth were to be more evenly distributed political organization, and the continuing necessity thereof, will always divide men into those who rule —those who have power and influence—and those who are ruled. Equality in respect of power, runs the argument, is unattainable; and if democracy either means or requires such equality then democracy too is for ever beyond our grasp.

In order to limit what could easily turn into a very wide-ranging discussion I propose to concentrate only on certain aspects of what is in dispute between Marxists and the school of élite theorists and I shall begin with a closer look at the Marxian theory of the state or, to be more precise, at the account given by Engels in his *Origin of the Family, Private Property and the State*.[6]

Engels maintains that the state is a product of certain developments in society at a particular stage in its evolution. It emerges because society has become divided into classes with conflicting economic interests and there is a need 'to moderate the conflict and keep it within the bounds of "order" '.[7] Normally, he says, the state is the instrument of the dominant economic class but he admits that there are 'exceptional periods' when the opposing classes are so evenly balanced that 'the state power, as apparent mediator, acquires for the moment a certain independence in relation to both'.[8] The normal situation, however, is one in which the group owning and controlling the means of production —and this is what constitutes it as a class—is able to use the state power to maintain its position. But developments in the advanced capitalist countries promised to bring about an entirely new situation. As Engels put it in a much quoted passage:

We are now rapidly approaching a stage in the development of production at which the existence of these classes has not only ceased to be a necessity, but becomes a positive hindrance to production. They will fall as inevitably as they once arose. The state inevitably falls with them. The society which organises production anew on the basis of free and equal association of the producers will put the whole state machinery where it will then belong—into the museum of antiquities, next the spinning wheel and the bronze axe.[9]

Engels' theory, as I have summarized it, is stated in broad terms and it would be unfair to insist that it should cover all the turns and twists of history. But one of its main contentions, that the state will disappear after, or along with, the abolition of classes, stands opposed to the view, not by any means restricted to élite theorists in the narrow sense, that society cannot do without a system of government involving authority, power, and coercion. Now, if the latter view is correct it would mean that a significant kind of inequality is unavoidable; and if we concede the more specific case of the élitists the nature of the inequality becomes heavily underlined.

A common reaction to Engels' forecast of the disappearance of the state has been to invoke the traditional assumption that some kind of government is a necessity in human society and to insist that especially in societies as complex as they had become in Engels' day public affairs cannot be managed without the type of decision-making, administrative, and judicial processes characteristic of the modern state. If Engels meant to imply that we could dispense with regulatory agencies of this kind then, it has been said, he must have supposed that human beings in the classless society would be so filled with concern for the common good that they would no longer need to be 'ruled'. And it must be admitted that there are passages in the classical Marxian texts which can bear this construction.

But Engels' position is rather more complex and (shall we say?) realistic than that of the anarcho-utopian; for he certainly did not believe that *all* authority, *all* mechanisms of administration and control, would become superfluous in the classless society. On the contrary, in a passage as much quoted as the one above, he states quite explicitly that certain forms of control would have to be maintained. Once class domination has been abolished, he says. 'there is nothing more to be repressed which would make a special repressive force, a state, necessary'. But, he goes on:

The first act in which the state really comes forward as the representative of society as a whole—the taking possession of the means of production in the name of society—is at the same time its last independent act as a state. The interference of the state power in social relations becomes superfluous in one sphere after another, and then ceases of itself. The government of persons is replaced by the administration of things and the direction of the processes of production.[10]

There are several problems facing anyone who wants to get at Engels' meaning in these passages. Not the least difficult of them arises from Engels' apparently unequivocal assertion that the state will disappear, or 'die off', and that production will be organized on the basis of the *free* and *equal* association of the producers. Yet he also speaks of the 'administration' of things and the 'direction' of the processes of production. Is it possible to talk of equality when there will continue to be 'administration' and '*direction*' in industry? It is true that one of his translators has rendered *Leitung* not as 'direction' but as 'conduct', thus enabling the impression to be created that the producers would indeed be associated on a free and equal basis. But this is to assign the mildest possible force to *Leitung*. Moreover such a rendering fails to accord with some very forthright remarks Engels made in an article criticizing those socialists who had 'latterly launched a regular crusade against what they call the *principle of authority*'. The conclusion at which Engels arrives in this article is that:

> . . . a certain authority, no matter how delegated, and, on the other hand, a certain subordination are things which, independent of all social organisation, are imposed upon us together with the material conditions under which we produce and make products circulate.[11]

By authority Engels means a relationship in which the will of one person is imposed upon another's, 'authority presupposes subordination'. The conditions under which production is carried on in modern industry, in the factories, on the railways, and even in agriculture, involve 'combined action' and, Engels maintains, this implies organization. Now can there be organization, he asks, without authority? Let us suppose the revolution to have overthrown the bourgeoisie: 'will authority have disappeared or will it only have changed its form?' The whole point of the article is to argue that authority will not, cannot, disappear. Yet Engels reiterates his conviction that 'the political state', 'political authority', will disappear. 'Public functions,' he says, 'will lose their political character and be transformed into the simple administrative functions of watching over the true interests of society.'[12]

In order to sustain Engels' thesis it would appear to be necessary to establish a viable distinction between the state as 'a special repressive force' and 'the administration of things' or 'the simple administrative functions of watching over the true interests of society'. Perhaps one should not be too pedantic here, but what sources does one have other than the actual wording in the texts? And in these Engels contrasts 'government of persons' and 'the interference of the state power in social relations' with 'the administration of things'. Now, from his own description, we learn that, in the management of industrial enterprises at least, 'authority' will continue to exist, with all that this implies in the way of inequality in working relationships. But the more important question, which has been asked many times, is: how can it be shown that the 'administration of things' will not involve the 'government of persons'? Does Engels mean we should assume that there will never be occasions when some person, or group of persons, will hold a different conception of the 'true interests of society' from those who are charged with watching over them?[13] That there will no longer be those fallible mortals who put personal gain before the social good? Or are we to assume that questions such as these simply cannot arise once class antagonisms have been abolished? Engels himself, however, seems to allow that conflicts of interest can occur without their having been generated by class divisions, as we shall see presently.

Moreover, the enormous advances in science and technology since Engels' time are constantly throwing up acute problems arising from the impact of industrial and commercial needs on human comfort and enjoyment, problems that have no special class significance and over which there can be serious conflicts of opinion. Is it not possible that we shall get more rather than fewer problems of this type? Will not the final decisions on, say, the location of new airports or power stations, on industrial claims on national parks, involve 'the government of persons' or 'the interference of the state power in social relations'? And would not those entrusted with the power to make such decisions, albeit dedicated to pursuing the 'true interests of society', be unequal, in respect of power and authority, as compared to those who would be forced to accept their decisions?

The difficulty about trying to extract answers to these questions from the classical Marxian texts is not merely that they do not attempt to offer detailed blueprints of the future Communist society; it arises at least as much from the way in which, while putting the main emphasis on the conception of the state as an instrument of class oppression, they acknowledge the need for 'public decisions' in any complex society, decisions which they would regard as necessary and legitimate yet lacking a 'political' and hence an oppressive character—thus the tendency to talk of 'political power properly so called'. In effect Marx and Engels say that, though for most of human history since the appearance of classes political power has been exercised for the advantage of the propertied classes, it has also been used for other purposes. Their theory is therefore more complex than a hasty reading of much-quoted passages is likely to suggest.

The main tendency in Marx and Engels, to repeat, is to identify the state ('a special repressive force') with the function of maintaining class domination. But it seems unlikely that they intended to *define* the state in terms of this function since, as we have seen, they allowed for 'exceptional periods' when the conflicting classes were so evenly balanced that the state manages to acquire a measure of independent power. And, as a matter of fact, apart from describing it as an instrument of class oppression ('the organized power of one class for oppressing another', as they say in the *Manifesto*[14]) we also come across a narrower definition of the state—as 'the government machine'.[15] This machine could, according to Marx, become a 'parasitic growth' on society and at the time of Louis Bonaparte, for instance, it did assume just such a character.

> All that France seems to have secured by the attempt to escape the despotism of a class is that she has had to surrender to the despotism of an individual . . . all classes alike, impotent and mute, have fallen on their knees before the rifle butt . . . [Succeeding revolutions have served to increase governmental power and] to the parties competing for dominion, the occupation of this huge state edifice has become the most important of the spoils of victory. . . . This executive, with its colossal bureaucratic and military organisation . . . this executive is a sort of dreadful parasitic growth, or a sort of network enwrapping the body and limbs and choking the pores of French sciety.[16]

Now it is important to appreciate that what Marx and Engels say about the state in such 'exceptional periods' is not a careless and unintended departure from their general theory of the nature of political power. Indeed, Engels' reference to these 'exceptional periods', cited above, occurs in a passage where he is dealing *generally* with the role of the state ('it is *normally* the state of the most powerful, economically ruling class . . .').[17] Moreover, in an exposition of historical materialism written in 1890 Engels stated:

> Society gives rise to certain common functions which it cannot dispense with. The persons selected for these functions form a new branch of the division of labour *within society*. This gives them particular interests, distinct too from the interests of those who gave them their office and—the state is in being.

Engels goes on to say that this new power acquires more 'independence' than that originally granted to it; it strives for 'as much independence as possible'; having been set up it is 'also endowed with a movement of its own', though, on the whole, 'the economic movement gets its way'.[18]

Part of the significance of this account lies in the idea of society having 'certain common functions', for the implication seems to be that the persons exercising state power have more than one role. On the one hand they are, normally, representatives of the dominant economic class whose interests they are there to protect; on the other hand they carry out certain activities that are indispensable to society. Furthermore they have particular interests of their own which, presumably, may or may not coincide with the exercise of indispensable social functions. I do not wish to suggest that these three roles are necessarily distinct on all occasions. My point is simply that Engels' account of political power makes it a more complex affair than is implied by the simple 'class instrument' version. As to the 'common functions' which Engels mentions, some idea of what he is referring to can be gained from certain passages in *Anti-Dühring*. He describes there the way society becomes divided into classes ('the privileged and the dispossessed, the exploiters and the exploited, the rulers and the ruled') and goes on to assert:

> . . . the state, which the primitive groups of communities of the same tribe had at first arrived at only for safeguarding their common interests . . . from this stage onwards acquires just as much the function of maintaining by force the economic and political position of the ruling class against the subject class.[19]

As examples of these 'common interests' he cites 'irrigation in the East' and defence against hostile outsiders. Later on in *Anti-Dühring* he says that in the very early stages of human society, before there were classes and when men lived in conditions of equality, there were from the start 'certain common interests' whose protection was in the hands of special individuals. These individuals, however, were under 'the control of the community as a whole'. And of these 'common interests' he mentions 'repression of encroachments by individuals on the rights of others', 'adjudication of disputes', 'control of water supplies, especially in hot countries', and 'religious functions'.[20] The individuals who engage in these activities are, he says, 'endowed with a certain measure of authority and the beginnings of state power'; gradually they make themselves more independent of the society whose common interests they were appointed to safeguard until they come to dominate it and constitute themselves a ruling class.[21]

So far as I know neither Marx nor Engels ever says that the need to safeguard certain 'common interests' will become superfluous under Communism. What they do envisage is that political rule, the 'government of persons', will disappear; that the exercise of certain indispensable social functions will lose its oppressive character. The distinction they make between 'administration of things' and 'government of persons' appears in somewhat different language in Marx's account of the Paris Commune in which he talks of the destruction of the 'merely repressive organs' of the old regime as opposed to the exercise of 'legitimate functions' which is to be restored to 'the responsible agents of society'.[22] Marx was not, of course, writing about Communist society but the language he uses undoubtedly derives from the distinction to which he and Engels seem to have been committed, namely, between what might be called 'social administration' and 'political rule' or 'political power properly so called'. And what lies behind the distinction is, in large part at least, the belief that since the main source of dissension in society will have been removed by the abolition of economic exploitation—as they define it—social problems can henceforth be tackled on their own merits, in a spirit of social solidarity, free from the distorting perspective of class interest.[23]

But the key question for us is whether social administration, as opposed to the 'government of persons', will involve relations of inequality. Our brief survey of their relevant writings does not take us very far since Marx and Engels leave the notion of 'the administration of things' largely unexplained, simply taking it for granted that coercion and oppression will cease to be necessary for the exercise of 'public functions'. On the other hand Engels is quite specific that, in large industrial enterprises at any rate, talk about the end of authority—and he makes it abundantly clear that 'authority presupposes subordination' —is absurd.

'It is absurd to speak of the principle of authority as being absolutely evil and of the principle of autonomy as being absolutely good,' he insists; what is required is that authority should be confined 'to the limits within which the conditions of production render it inevitable'.[24]

Now Engels was writing about the conditions of production in large-scale industry and agriculture (incidentally, how large does the scale have to be before conditions require the exercise of authority?) but his remarks are clearly applicable to any large-scale organization. Public service departments dealing with such matters as health, education, and protection of the environment, in fact all branches of the welfare state bureaucracy which manage to survive into the new era, would presumably have to be organized on the same principle. So, unless I have seriously misunderstood him, it would appear that, in Engels' view, working relationships for a substantial part, if not most, of the working population will be subject to authority and hence, in the strict sense, unequal. It may well be that Engels was less dismayed at such a prospect than Marx. His criticism of those who took the demand for equality too far seems on the whole to be more emphatic and persistent than anything we can find in his partner; and it is an attitude which seems hard to reconcile with his conviction that the future Communist society would be one of 'the free and equal association of producers'.[25]

The phrase, 'the administration of things', conveys the impression, perhaps intentionally, that all problems in Communist society will be purely administrative and/or technical ones. People will be agreed about ends and basic social purposes and so the questions to be dealt with will be instrumental, requiring the application of expert knowledge within a context of common values. Inequality, on this version, need therefore be taken no further than the requirements of production in industry and agriculture, and the organizational needs of the public services. But if within particular organizations some kind of hierarchy and the observance of certain rules and practices will continue to be necessary, would there not be the need for a similar structure in the arrangements for making public decisions, carrying on public functions and settling public policy? If regard for the common good and a high sense of public responsibility are by themselves not enough to ensure the efficient running of industry and have therefore to be supplemented by the exercise of authority, would not the same apply, perhaps to a smaller degree, to the arrangements for the conduct of public affairs? There can be no doubt that both Marx and Engels thought there would be matters of common concern in Communist society and that certain persons would exercise continuing roles, subject to procedures of democratic control, in attending to 'the true interests of society'. I added the qualification, 'to a smaller degree', because, although what are called 'consultation' and 'worker-participation' would presumably become important features in an industrial organization, the scope for democratic procedures may not be as great as in the election and control of public officials and representatives.

Now if there are to be public officials ('servants', 'agents' or what you will) acting in socially approved roles then, in respect of the functions they perform as administrators and/or adjudicators, they will clearly be entrusted with power and authority. And on the face of it this must surely mean that their activities could result in some persons being coerced and oppressed, at least as we normally use these terms. But, as we have seen, Marx and Engels gave a special meaning to these terms such that with the disappearance of 'political power properly so called' (or 'the government of persons') coercion and oppression would also come to an end.

However, whether or not a viable case can be made out for saying that the political, or coercive, aspect of carrying on public functions will disappear, the evidence seems to me to suggest that Marx and Engels did not think of Communist society as one in which there would be, in its literal sense, political equality. And I say this mainly because the very fact that there will be 'public functions', granting democratic control and unity of moral outlook on basic principles, constitutes in itself a means of differentiating between those who do and those who do not have the authority to exercise these functions; to which might be added the 'unofficial' influence that various particular individuals exercise in many walks of life, but especially when men come to consider public policy and make decisions thereon.

It may well be objected that, relying mainly on some passages in Engels, I have overstated the extent to which Marx would have condoned authority, hence political inequality, in Communist society. I have already admitted this possibility.[26] On the other hand, as I have insistently stressed, neither Marx nor Engels goes into much detail about life in Communist society and we have no more to rely on than the few hints scattered here and there in their writings. But, I repeat, they say enough to justify the conclusion that they envisage a society in which public functions are performed and in which there are public policies; and that therefore there must be procedures for arriving at these policies and for carrying them out. All of which, for reasons stated, implies political inequality. And this is quite consistent with the importance they attach to removal of the coercive and oppressive features of political authority, which they believed would follow from the abolition of classes and the ending of alienation for man as producer.

It is possible that on the issue of authority in Communist society Engels differed from Marx as much as some commentators have claimed he did. Robert C. Tucker, for example, takes Engels' article 'On Authority' to be an implicit contradiction of 'Marx's vision of the factory of the future as a realm of freedom in the life of production . . . [for] a nonauthoritarian existence in the factory was integral to communism itself in Marx's understanding of it . . .'[27] Tucker argues from the premise that Marx adopted the anarchist view of the state, namely, that the state was an obstacle to, and inconsistent with, the attainment of freedom, and that freedom was for him 'the supreme human value'. Tucker allows however, that Marx anticipated there would still be 'certain functions of public administration' and 'direction of the process of production' in the higher phase of Communist society. But, he says, these functions would not be performed 'by a state in Marx's definition of the term', i.e. 'a special organism separated from society through the division of labour'.[28]

Tucker's remarks raise several important issues about the Marxian vision of the future society. Let us deal first with the apparent conflict between Marx and Engels on the question of authority. We should notice that Tucker has both Marx and Engels agreeing on the need for 'certain functions of public administration' and for 'direction of the process of production'. Now I should have thought that if these expressions were used with any care they would in themselves have carried the consequence of some considerable degree of authority in industrial production and public administration.

Tucker cannot see Marx accepting what Engels says about the need for authority in large-scale industry, but Marx wrote something very similar to Engels on this very topic, as we have already had occasion to remark. There is a passage in the third volume of *Capital* where he writes of the need to co-ordinate and unify the process of production in a workshop and compares the 'commanding will' required for this task, 'which must be performed in every mode of production', with the conductor of an orchestra.[29] He also mentions a wider co-ordinating function which has to be performed in respect of 'the common operations arising from the nature of all communities'.[30] And in view of the enormous importance that both he and Engels attached to 'planned production', as opposed to the arbitrary working of market forces under capitalism, the role of the 'co-ordinators' in this sphere would clearly be crucial. So I am inclined to think that, though there is much in Marx which corresponds to what Tucker attributes to him, the alleged conflict between him and Engels over the role of authority in Communist society has been greatly exaggerated. Marx's denunciations of political authority can easily mislead his readers into thinking that he was quite unrealistic about the organizational requirements of higher Communism. But there are unmistakable signs that he agreed with Engels on the continuing need for authority of some kind both within large-scale industrial units and in the wider co-ordinating functions affecting a whole society.

When Tucker says that the functions of public administration and directing the processes of production would not, according to Marx, be performed by the state, conceived as 'a special organism separated from society through the division of labour', he is in effect raising some very pertinent questions about the whole character of 'administration' in a Communist society—will there, for example, be a professional corps of public officials?—and, in particular, whether it could be said that public officials may have to resort to 'coercion' in the course of carrying out public policy. For the idea of public administration being carried on by persons who are *not* separated from society by the division of labour seems to be a way of saying that there will *not* be a professional corps of public servants.

Certainly the existence of a permanent bureaucracy with powers of coercion in the execution of public policy is hard to reconcile with political equality, even if that policy could be said to emanate from the will of a people freed from the shackles of class rule. Moreover, a permanent bureaucracy would be inconsistent with the practice of everyone taking a hand at public administration, a suggestion designed both to widen the range of men's activities and to democratize the administrative process. If things could indeed be so arranged that we all took a turn, somewhat as people are drawn into party work at elections, the gulf between administrators and administered would be considerably narrowed, maybe even disappear, and it would then seem plausible to talk about the 'government of persons' giving way to 'the administration of things', about the end of coercion and oppression. There must surely be many who do not regard themselves as revolutionary Marxists who would nevertheless find this a very attractive idea, especially those who have a strong predilection for putting curbs on the bureaucratic monster by every available means. In this way too substance would be given to Marx's aim of abolishing the state as an *alien force* and of man becoming, and feeling that he is, the master of his fate.

But, alas! what Marx and Engels say about the need for authority and co-ordination, together with what is implied in the *planning* of production, go against the notion that public administration can be an 'amateur' activity. Since the time of Marx's death we have become even more aware of the enormous demand for highly skilled specialists at various levels and in many sectors of an industrial economy, and it is difficult to believe that, however well educated we may all become, we could literally turn our hands to anything. Narrow specialization can be an evil, though I do not see why we should either be contemptuous of, or try to stop a man from, restricting himself to, say, research in chemistry and playing the piano. But admirable though we think it is that a man should widen his horizons and be able to engage in many kinds of activity, the idea that it could be open to anyone to acquire the range of skills and degree of expert knowledge to fit him for responsible work in any branch of industry or public administration is very hard to accept.

There is, however, lurking in the background a more fundamental question that ought to be asked about the 'administration of things'. It might be argued that though there has to be authority and co-ordination, and that this makes for inequalities in the strict sense (i.e. people would differ in respect of power, authority, and influence), what matters is that such differences should not be oppressive, should not involve coercion. There are, after all, differences of this character in sporting teams, in scientific research units and among the members of an orchestra. These are not examples of unwilling subordination or of oppressive relationships. It is when inequalities create barriers between people, when they involve coercion, that they smack of 'government' as opposed to 'administration'.

I hesitate to start discussing 'coercion' or to enquire whether coercion will be necessary when classes have been abolished, but my survey of the Marxian attitude to political equality has reached a stage where it cannot be avoided. So far, the factors making for authority and the observance of regulations have been connected with the productive process: according to Marx and Engels they will play a necessary role within organizations and also in securing co-ordination between them, i.e. in the economy as a whole. Did Marx and Engels imagine that these processes would be 'purely administrative', giving rise to no important issues of *policy*?

The phrase 'the administration of things' (as I have already suggested) does tend to create this impression. But what if there were serious disagreements (dare I call them 'conflicts of interest'?) about the allocation of resources? For example, could there not be disagreements of this type during the discussions leading to the formulation of an over-all plan for the economy? And might not such disagreements correspond to differences of opinion in the wider society about the scale of priorities in allocating capital resources, and not be just confined to the experts concerned with planning and co-ordination?

To these questions one possible answer is that with the end of classes and exploitation there will be no disagreements on basic principles but only over means.* Surely, here, the proper reaction is to ask, first of all, *how* could anyone know, or have reason to believe, of a *future* society that there will never be disagreements in it on matters of principle? Such evidence as is available to us comes only from societies which, although they have had Marxist rulers for some decades, are still very far from entering the stage of 'higher Communism'. And this evidence is decisively negative. On the other hand it would be quite useless to try to make it all a matter of definition: that is, by Communism is *meant* a society without clashes of principle and hence having no need for coercion. Such a definition could not count as a reason for predicting the actual existence of such a society.

Thus, to acquire even initial plausibility the answer would have to rely on empirical evidence of some kind; or at least to involve an appeal to empirical considerations of an indirect sort. And I suppose the standard Marxist reply, somewhat simplified, would be that moral beliefs and attitudes, political principles and principles of social policy, all have a relative character since they are generated by and function within the mode of production prevailing in any particular epoch. Once, therefore, the last antagonistic form of the mode of production has given way to social ownership and control of the means of production class divisions will disappear and along with them the ideological, including the moral, elements associated with the dominant classes of the past. In their place there will emerge a new morality, a secular humanism, which takes as its fundamental objective the satisfaction of the real *needs* of man and the fulfilment of the potentialities of all members of society.

* I must confess that this answer, implicit in Marx and Engels and very explicit in some of their followers[31]—an answer that certainly helps to make sense of the 'government of persons' giving way to the 'administration of things' —is so far-reaching in its assumptions that I feel almost helpless to deal with it.

In *The German Ideology* Marx and Engels write of 'an all-round development of individuals' and say that only in Communist society can there be any serious talk of 'the original and free development of individuals'. In the *Manifesto* they predict the replacement of bourgeois society by an association 'in which the free development of each is the condition for the free development of all'.[32] Out of pronouncements of this kind a number of Marxists have in recent decades been attempting to fashion a humanist morality based on 'human needs', and the assumption one often comes across—an assumption by no means confined to Marxists—is that needs are those things among all the desires and wants of human beings which right-thinking and/or rational persons would agree upon as legitimate and hence worthy of satisfaction.

What seems to be ruled out is that rational persons could either disagree about what is to be included among human needs, or about their relative importance; for if the possibility of disagreement on either or both of these counts is allowed, the assumption of agreement on basic principles among the members of Communist society is hard to sustain. Yet in the world as we know it there certainly are many disagreements of this sort: could it be shown that the source of these disagreements is always the class position of the contending parties or that the respective viewpoints are always generated by class interests? Even in the case of such basic requirements as food and shelter there is no unanimity on their *relative* importance. Every rational person does assuredly believe that these requirements ought to be satisfied in the case of *all* men, as soon as possible and as a matter of great urgency. Yet there are countries where the rulers, apparently with a good deal of support from their subjects, subordinate the satisfaction of these needs to considerations of 'national security' or national prestige. In a world where so much has to be done to meet elementary needs for food, clothing, shelter, education, and health enormous sums are spent on armaments, space projects, and supersonic aircraft with, it is claimed, the approval of the needy themselves.

When we move from what would be widely accepted as basic or elementary needs to the more complex things which would be required to ensure 'the fullest possible development of man's limitless potentialities' or 'the full flowering of the personality' the chances of finding agreement among all 'rational' persons seems even more remote.[33] Moreover, the obstacles to agreement would not be a matter of the remnants of class interest distorting the demands of Communist man, as opposed to bourgeois ethics *v.* proletarian ethics.

Where the belief in the moral homogeneity of Communist society goes wrong is in its failure to recognize that what is to count as a need is not a purely scientific or empirical question, that the problem of what to include in a list of needs (let us grant that everyone would agree on the basic ones already mentioned in this chapter) depends on what one thinks is important in life. And that is not an empirical or scientific matter. I do not see much of a case for assuming that once classes have been abolished men's views on what is important will always coincide; or for saying that when they do not coincide it is a question of the rational and the sane against the blind and the pathological. Eugene Kamenka has neatly summed up this kind of Marxist writing:

> There is a clear assumption of a life 'proper to man', constantly appealed to but quite inadequately discussed . . . Allied with this is the distinction, common in Marxist propaganda, between real 'needs' and mere irrational desires. Morality, in other words, is based on what men want, but we are to include only their rational, real (read approved?) wants.[34]

Exactly what kinds of differences would exist in a non-class society (in the Marxian sense)—different interest groups, differences in moral outlook and in political principle—and which of them would involve coercion (or oppression, for that matter) it is plainly absurd to try to predict. Indeed, it is when one tries to construct imaginatively a society of this type in order to see what sorts of differences there would be and how people would go about settling them, that it becomes evident how near to a claim to omniscience is the prediction that there will be no disagreements in interest or principle under Communism.

The question of the possibility of coercion in the classless society has been discussed so far without stopping to ask what is meant by 'coercion'; and the same would apply to 'oppression'. Nor would it follow that, even if there were to be moral homogeneity and agreement on principles, there would be no important differences requiring appropriate means and methods for resolving them, for men who agree on principles often disagree on how to interpret and apply them. It might, for example, be agreed that preservation of the countryside was a high priority, yet in particular cases there could well be serious differences about the best means to achieve the goal or over what parts of the countryside were most worth preserving. Similar problems could arise over the allocation of resources for extremely expensive projects such as space exploration. Some general formula indicating the relative importance of space exploration and roads or education might be widely assented to and yet give rise to differences over its interpretation and application. Now, is Communist society to be free of dissension on issues of this kind? No one but a romantic utopian could be sure of an affirmative answer to this question.

To return to coercion. I have already rejected the suggestion that, because classes and exploitation have been abolished, there will be no coercion in a Communist society. Coercion can be exercised in various ways (and there can be various forms of oppression too), and if a Marxist really wishes to demonstrate the impossibility of any form of coercion in a certain future society he can only do so by a definitional manoeuvre rather than on the basis of what is foreseeable in an empirical way.

There can be coercion in the shape of general laws whose breach can be the subject of proceedings and punishment in official courts. Provided these courts are conducted fairly and humanely I can imagine many people preferring to face them rather than risk 'people's justice' in the 'neighbourhood' or 'comradely' courts that Marxists have sometimes favoured. Then there can be rules with a restricted application, relating to one's place of work or to any one of the innumerable associations to which men belong, together with procedures for adjudication in case of violation thereof. There is also the moral pressure of public opinion; fear of the disapproval of one's fellows can be a restraining influence on one's conduct. In all these ways, and many others too numerous to deal with here, we can be coerced.[35]

Now when coercion in any one or more of its various forms is applied to uphold rules and practices which manifest values or policies one strongly disapproves of, no matter how fair or 'comradely' the procedure, it is still coercion. And it could be felt as oppressive. Furthermore it is no less coercion if the rules have the solid backing of the great majority of people and are being administered and enforced by the 'responsible agents of society'. From what Marx and Engels say about the need for authority and coercion it is difficult to see how the use of coercion could be avoided—except, of course, on the assumption which we have already considered, namely, that there will be such a high degree of moral homogeneity as to make coercion superfluous. But if coercion is necessary then the arrangements which must accompany some of its forms look very much like what we normally understand by 'government'—not that it has to be precisely the same as we are familiar with in the contemporary world.

So we come back to the distinction between 'the government of persons' and 'the administration of things'. What, in the light of our survey, *is* the distinction? The balance of the argument points to the continuing existence of authority, power, and coercion, and on any reasonable understanding of these terms, that implies inequality. Perhaps the use of the two phrases was chiefly designed to indicate a substantial difference in the extent and amount of coercion as between class and classless societies. It may turn out that in a Communist society popular participation and democratic control over officials can be combined with a genuine respect for minority interests so that government is no longer felt to be a distant and alien force. Thus on a charitable reading of the course of development to be expected from the abolition of classes the role of coercion would be significantly less prominent in Communist society.[36] Even so we could not be 'free and equal' in the strict sense of the terms. Indeed to make men literally so is surely part of no one's purpose. For there can be no society where men are entirely free; nor one where all men are equally possessed of power and authority.

6/Equality and Elites

Part of what is meant by saying that man is a political animal is that relationships of power and authority have always been characteristic of the human situation. It is one of the concerns of political theory to determine when government, or a political system, can be said to exist; whether relationships of power and authority are both necessary and sufficient for the existence of a political system. Robert A. Dahl, for example, is prepared to define a political system as 'any persistent pattern of human relationships that involves, to a significant extent, power, rule, or authority'.[1]

The great majority of political thinkers whose names figure in the histories of the subject, and most contemporary political theorists in the English-speaking world, say, or would say, that relationships of this sort have indeed always been a feature of human societies. And I fancy that most of them would also go on to say that there is little prospect of it being otherwise. To speak thus is, of course, to speak in general terms and in no way settles the type and degree of power and authority which future societies will manifest. Nor does it resolve the questions that arise about early forms of human society, so-called primitive man. Most anthropologists would say that human societies everywhere, at any time, have systems of 'social control'. Thus John Beattie:

> There could be no coherent social life unless the social relationships which bind people together were at least to some degree orderly, institutionalized and predictable . . . To maintain an orderly system of social relations people have to be subjected to some degree of compulsion . . . The exercise of some form of legitimized or authorized social power, or the possibility of its exercise, appears generally to be a condition of the maintenance of social order.[2]

Is this the same as saying that *government* is a necessary condition of 'coherent social life'? R. M. MacIver is quite explicit about it: 'Government is the organisation of men under authority . . . Wherever man lives on earth, at whatever level of existence, there is social order, and always permeating it is government of some sort. Government is an aspect of society.'[3]

A common reason advanced for this alleged universal phenomenon of government is that men have desires, wants, and interests which compete and conflict with one another; that men also differ in their attitudes, in the principles they subscribe to and on matters of policy—though this way of putting it applies perhaps to man only in the later phases of his history. The bearing of all this on political equality and on the Marxist idea of an end to government should be obvious. Because, it is claimed, men *do* have conflicting interests and divergent aims, and will continue to have them in the foreseeable future, some means for avoiding or settling disputes must be provided; and this means government. To quote Dahl again:

> If everyone were perfectly agreed on ends and means, no one would ever need to change the way of another. Hence no relations of influence or power would arise. Hence no political system would exist. Let one person frustrate another in the pursuit of his goals and you already have the germ of a political system . . . Conflict and politics are born inseparable twins.[4]

The existence of government implies inequality because government consists of a set of arrangements whereby some individuals are authorized and have the power to control the actions of others. Whether or not the authorization is conferred in a democratic manner it involves the possession of varying degrees of influence and power by those who have been appointed or elected to public office. And even when we include people with no office or role in governmental institutions, who wield substantial though varying degrees of power and influence in the activity which is directed at those institutions, we still have a small minority of the total population. As Lasswell and Kaplan put it in their very influential book, *Power and Society*: 'Power is never equally distributed: there is always an élite . . . If political equality were defined so as to exclude the existence of an élite, the concept would be vacuous.'[5] What is important, they go on to say, is the manner in which the élite is recruited; whether 'recruitment is based on values to which there is equal access', quoting a passage from Tawney's *Equality* in support.

The fact that Lasswell and Kaplan can invoke Tawney's name in this connection is significant, for Tawney was a dedicated egalitarian who nonetheless saw that there were limits to what could be distributed equally. The context of the passage is therefore worth our attention. It comes in the second chapter of *Equality*, where Tawney argues that the ideal of equality does not rest on 'the romantic illusion that men are equal in character and intelligence' but rather on the conviction that 'individual differences, which are a source of social energy, are more likely to ripen and find expression if social inequalities are, so far as practicable, diminished'.[6] English society, he says, is hierarchical and it establishes its gradations not in terms of function but of wealth. Thus it is not only pyramidal in structure, as are all social systems, but the layers in the pyramid reflect less the differences of character and ability than differences of social class; it is a hierarchy which puts more emphasis on those qualities in respect of which discrimination is unjustified and less on those related 'to varying levels of human capacity'.[7]

This is the setting of the passage quoted by Lasswell and Kaplan:

> All forms of social organization are hierarchical, in the sense that they imply *gradations of responsibility and power*, which vary from individual to individual according to his place in the system. But these *gradations* may be *based on differences of function and office*, may relate only to those aspects of life which are relevant to such differences, and may be compatible with the easy movement of individuals, according to their capacity, from one point on the scale to another. Or they may have their source in differences of birth, or wealth, or social position . . .[8]

The point Tawney goes on to make is that 'the necessary diversity' of function in social organizations is compatible with a large measure of economic and social equality. Gradations of responsibility and power can go along with roughly equal standards in, say, the provision of health and education services, with equal immunity 'from the more degrading forms of poverty' and equal security against 'economic oppression'.[9]

When Lasswell and Kaplan assert that power is never equally distributed, that 'there is always an élite', they are not necessarily committing themselves to the type of élite theory advocated by Michels, whose thesis was briefly referred to in the last chapter. Indeed the extracts from Bluntschli and Bryce which they quote in support of their claim say no more than that the distinction between rulers and ruled 'is always necessary', that the power of decision in all forms of government is always in the hands of the few, 'though in different degrees'.[10]

Now the debate stimulated by élite theory has shown how essential it is to try to differentiate between the oft-made assertion that there will always be a distinction between rulers and ruled and the much stronger looking claim that the power of decision is always in the hands of an élite. Is it not important to take account of the 'different degrees' here? Does it not matter whether the rulers have to operate within a framework of institutions which imposes checks on their activities and ensures a high degree of responsibility to a freely voting electorate? Whether regular elections and/or referenda, and certain standards of public life, set significant limits to their power of decision? If these restraints do make a difference and therefore some force can be assigned to the notion of democratic responsibility—maybe not realized yet in sufficient measure in the liberal-democratic regimes of the world—then much of the sting is drawn out of the apparently inexorable character of élite rule to which Michels and others have for ever consigned us.

As Dahl observes, from the fact that 'control over political resources is distributed unevenly' one should not conclude that variations in the manner of their distribution in different societies are unimportant.[11] There are times when Michels recognizes this, but mostly he is concerned to assert and reassert 'the iron law of oligarchy', a law which, as J. H. Meisel has put it, 'operates in all human associations, rendering all democratic aspirations illusory'.[12]

At the end of Michels' celebrated work, *Political Parties*, in which he attempts to show that the oligarchical tendencies inherent in every large-scale organization invariably defeat the claims of democracy and equality, Michels confesses that 'it is none the less true that as a form of life we must choose democracy as the least of evils' and warns that 'nothing but a serene and frank examination of the oligarchical dangers of democracy will enable us to minimize these dangers, even though they can never be entirely avoided'. He tells the story of the dying peasant who informs his sons of a treasure buried in the field:

> After the old man's death the sons dig everywhere in order to discover the treasure. They do not find it. But their indefatigable labour improves the soil and secures for them a comparative well-being. The treasure in the fable may well symbolize democracy. Democracy is a treasure which no one will ever discover by deliberate search. But in continuing our search, in labouring indefatigably to discover the indiscoverable, we shall perform a work which will have fertile results in the democratic sense.[13]

In his *Political Parties* at least Michels does not adopt an anti-democratic position. At the outset he says that his principal aim is to

gain and promote *understanding* of the tendencies which stand in the
way of democracy; tendencies which arise from the nature of man,
from the nature of political struggle and from the nature of organization. In saying that 'democracy leads to oligarchy' he intends no moral
judgement either way, nor does he wish to level the charge of hypocrisy
at those who believe that democracy is attainable; for 'the law that it is
an essential characteristic of all human aggregates to constitute cliques
and sub-classes is, like every other sociological law, beyond good and
evil.'[14] The main burden of his argument is that the necessities of
large-scale organization bring about the rule of an élite, and from a
study of movements and parties which proclaim the ideal of equality he
comes to the conclusion that they, no less than parties with openly
élitist principles, fall under the domination of the few. This, for him,
constitutes 'conclusive proof of the existence of immanent oligarchical
tendencies in every kind of human organisation which strives for the
attainment of definite ends'.[15]

The principles of democracy, says Michels, guarantee to everyone an
equal influence and an *equal* participation in the affairs of the community.
But this is impossible. Democracy in this sense is at most applicable
only on a very small scale. The issues that arise for decision in any large
organization cannot be dealt with by every member in that organization; delegation is unavoidable. Organization by its very nature implies
the tendency to oligarchy and the increase in the power of leaders is
proportional to the extension of the organization. Moreover technical
and administrative considerations make for specialization and promote
the development of an expert leadership. At the same time the masses
lack a sustained interest in public affairs; they cannot do without leadership, direction, and guidance. According to Marxist theory, élite rule
and the apathy of the masses is the product of class society, but when
the proletariat has put an end to the state the administration of the
economy will alone make for an extensive bureaucracy: 'we are led by
an inevitable logic to the flat denial of the possibility of a state without classes'. For the leaders of the proletariat will turn out to have
been:

> . . . sufficiently astute and sufficiently powerful to grasp the
> sceptre of dominion in the name of socialism, and to wrest it
> from the hands of the expiring bourgeois society . . . [they will]
> replace the visible and tangible dominant classes which now
> exist and act openly by a clandestine demagogic oligarchy, pur-
> suing its ends under the cloak of equality . . . The socialists

might conquer, but not socialism, which would perish in the moment of its adherents' triumph.[16]

This strikes Michels as a 'tragicomedy in which the masses are content to devote all their energies to effecting a change of masters'.[17] To those socialists who predict that a new social order will restore the people to health, provide them with a capacity for self-government, Michels replies that the 'immaturity of the mass' is not a temporary phenomenon because it 'derives from the very nature of mass as mass'.[18] Michels' thesis may therefore be summarized in an oft-quoted passage: 'It is organization which gives birth to the dominion of the elected over the electors, of the mandatories over the mandators, of the delegates over the delegators. Who says organization, says oligarchy'.[19]

And yet, implacable and unrelenting though all this seems, a ray of democratic light is permitted to shine through the oligarchical darkness; for the labour movement tends to generate a capacity for 'criticism and control' and produces 'a certain number of free spirits . . . never weary of asking the eternal "Why?" about every human institution'. The spread of education may reasonably be expected to extend this capacity, thus enabling the masses 'within the limits of what is possible' to counter-act the tendency toward oligarchy.[20]

To those who are regarded as the 'classical' exponents of democracy the assertion that power is always distributed unequally would have come as no surprise. James Mill, for example, advocated *representative* government precisely because the idea of equal influence and participation in the processes of government was patently absurd. What was important for him was that the rulers should be made responsive to, and promote the interests of, their subjects; and he thought, perhaps mistakenly, that the institutions of parliamentary democracy would secure this objective.

In recent decades many writers have sought to revise the classical version of democracy, in which government was required to reflect the will of the people, by portraying it as a competitive struggle among élites for the approval of the electorate. Although this idea suggests the influence of élite theorists such as Michels, it differs from theirs in a number of important ways. The few who have preponderant power are not treated as a monolithic group with largely identical beliefs and interests (Michels in particular has been charged with using the term 'oligarchy' to refer to several distinct entities, thus creating the impression of a solid unity among the powerful few[21]). And of those who compete openly for electoral support the very fact that they are rivals for the voters' favour is taken to constitute an effective limit to the exercise of power. Hence, provided the range of alternatives presented to the electorate corresponds to the principal divisions of interest in society, that these interests are articulated by a variety of intermediate groups, and that there is freedom for potential élites to enter the field and set up in competition, then the capacity for 'criticism and control', which Michels mentions almost as an afterthought, is given substantial form.

Thus, so far from the emergence of a single and solid bloc exercising a dominant role, the existence of a set of alternative élites is said to draw interests into coherent expression, to prevent a monopolistic concentration of power at the apex of the political pyramid, and to offer meaningful choices to the voters. The fact that élites occupy a key position in the democratic polity is not regarded by the exponents of 'democratic élitism' as a defect to be remedied; on the contrary, to quote Giovanni Sartori, one of the leading advocates of the theory, a democratic political system is one that makes the government 'responsive and accountable' and its effectiveness 'depends first and foremost on the efficiency and skill of its leadership'.[22]

The prospect for political equality is therefore bleak in both the full-blooded élitism of Michels and the theory of plural élites in contemporary political science. Naturally enough the radical egalitarian has raised his voice in protest. He requires of democracy that it really take its traditional commitment to equality seriously. For him the democratic élitist is too much of an élitist and not enough of a democrat. Peter Bachrach, for example, asks whether the interests of the people are properly satisfied by a system of plural élites. Have not contemporary analysts of democracy allowed their 'profound distrust of the majority of ordinary men and women' to turn what purports to be a purely explanatory model of present realities into a normative doctrine which seeks to remove political equality, in any meaningful sense, from its rightful place in the theory of democracy? Echoing J. S. Mill, he stresses the 'personal satisfaction and growth attained from active engagement in the political process' and argues that 'the full development of the personalities of adult men and women requires the opportunity and challenge to participate in public life beyond the ballot box and dues collection'.[23]

Bachrach does not maintain that what Mosca called 'absolute political equality' is an attainable goal. But though strict equality of political power is 'a utopian objective' ('. . . obviously in large societies "key governmental decisions" must be made by a few individuals') it surely does not follow that an ideal of this kind is without value.[24] Could it not serve as a goal towards which to move and a yardstick for measuring existing arrangements even if in its fullest sense we recognize it to be unrealizable? He therefore pleads for its retention both as an ideal for action and a criterion of judgement. He argues that there is a wide field of application for the concept of equality of power in the form of participation in local community affairs, in industrial enterprises, in issues which directly affect people in their places of residence and of work; though he concedes that, in the large corporation at least, 'some form of hierarchy' would still be necessary. The crucial problem for democracy, in Bachrach's view, is not the membership of the élite, it is whether

> . . . democracy can diffuse power sufficiently throughout society to inculcate among people in all walks of life a justifiable feeling that they have the power to participate in decisions which affect themselves and the common life of the community, especially the immediate community in which they work and spend most of their waking hours and energy . . .[25]

T. B. Bottomore is another for whom equality is intrinsic to the idea of democracy. Like Bachrach, he considers its importance and meaning have become diluted by contemporary political science, partly because of the alleged implications of the empirical evidence concerning the inevitability of élite power. Democracy, he says, means that 'there should be a substantial degree of equality among men' so that every adult, 'as far as is possible', can exercise an equal influence on the decisions which have an important bearing on the life of his society. And this requires the absence of those inequalities in wealth, status, education, and 'access to knowledge' which lead to 'the permanent subordination of some groups of men to others' in various spheres of social life.[26]

Bottomore is confident that we could achieve an equality of this kind because the major inequalities he sees in the world 'are in the main social products' and hence not natural. A pointer to the nature of his egalitarian sympathies is in his claim that Marx's notion of a classless society 'presents the ideal of equality in a form which is more widely accepted than any other in the modern world', but though Marx's goal constitutes the standard for his own conception of equality he admits to a crucial dilemma. Marx did not foresee the possibility of different sorts of social distinctions, even 'a new ruling class', emerging after the overthrow of capitalism. The lessons of the Stalinist era therefore lead Bottomore to urge the widest possible diffusion of political authority by conferring the power of decision, 'wherever feasible', upon local bodies and voluntary associations and by the introduction of self-government in industry. He is sensitive to the charge that the search for equality via the centralized state will threaten intellectual freedom and induce cultural conformity. He insists, therefore, that in 'the intellectual sphere it is particularly important that there should be independent associations which compete with each other'; not only in radio, television and the press but also in scholarly research and the publication of books. All of which he is sure can be achieved within the context of public ownership.[27]

With regard to the nature and extent of authority, influence, and power in the classless, egalitarian, society to which Bottomore looks forward, one is inclined to press the same sorts of questions as have already been raised in connection with Marx and Engels. Speaking of the 'independent associations' he would like to see operating in the intellectual sphere, he says that they would be 'owned or effectively controlled by their members', financed largely out of public funds and 'subject to general regulation by a national authority'. In industry and commerce he envisages the same sort of arrangement; the individual enterprises would be owned, 'and most of their policies decided upon', by those working in them, but they would be 'subject to controls of various kinds in the interests of a national economic plan'.[28] In these spheres, at least, there would be some form of national government with jurisdiction over the whole society. Presumably the problems of the allocation of land resources and environmental planning which have come increasingly to the fore in advanced industrial countries will still demand attention in the future and it would seem to be the sense of Bottomore's argument that these problems too would fall under the jurisdiction of national and local authorities.

He is not explicit about the 'key governmental decisions' at national level which Bachrach insists must always be taken by the few, but it is abundantly clear that decision-making processes, involving public bodies and officials with the right to carry out decisions, will operate in the classless society. And though he postulates a 'fundamental agreement among the members of society upon the general features of its organisation' and puts forward the demand that the individual should be 'freed from domination by a remote, inaccessible and unaccountable government and administration', there is nothing to suggest that he contemplates the disappearance of government as such.[29] Indeed, in the course of a discussion of the élite theories of Pareto and Mosca, he dismisses their claim that all societies in the past have been divided into rulers and ruled as a 'somewhat trivial observation', with the apparent implication that an egalitarian would not seek an end to this division beyond the point where everyone could 'participate as fully as possible in deciding issues of general social importance'.[30] What shape government would take, whether for instance there would be a permanent bureaucracy, is not explored in any detail apart from a declaration in favour of decentralization and a reference to Marx's praise for the Paris Commune, in which 'the functions of government were undertaken by municipal councillors, chosen by universal suffrage, responsible and revocable at short term'.[31]

The radical egalitarian's search for ways to make equality an effective and operative ideal in the political arrangements of the classless society stems from a conviction that each person should, as far as is possible, help shape his own destiny. A centralized and dominating government, dependent only on the periodical necessity of facing a mass electorate, seems to him to be too remote and inaccessible for the individual to have, and to feel that he has, any sort of capacity to participate significantly in deciding common social problems. But there is also the conviction that men should not be so unequally placed as to have appreciably different chances of developing their potentialities to the full, of which the right to share in political decision-making is a major facet.

Yet, in the case of writers such as Bachrach and Bottomore at any rate, it is not assumed that government can be dispensed with; and where there is government there is also inequality in the distribution of power, influence, and authority. They seem to talk at times as if strict equality in respect of these attributes would be worth having if it were attainable, but recognize that it is unattainable. For if some sort of government is taken to be a necessity for coping with various social problems, that in itself constitutes an obstacle to strict equality.

Is not the very idea of all men being equally possessed of authority and influence difficult to conceive? I do not mean, as Bachrach puts it, that 'the exigencies of life in the industrial and nuclear age necessitate that key and crucial political decisions in a democracy, as in totalitarian societies, be made by a handful of men',[32] but rather that, for example, if there is authority at all, i.e. the right to issue directives or to make binding decisions, it makes no sense to say that it is equally distributed. And there is no reason why all forms of authority should be regarded as a denial of one's own individuality or a restriction on one's capacity for development—any more than the influence of an artist or a philosopher should be taken thus. What Bottomore seems mainly to be after is the elimination of what to radical egalitarians appear as 'oppressive' forms of inequality, relationships of domination and exploitation, deprivation of some for the benefit of others, especially those conventional differences in wealth, status, and power which have the effect of cutting some groups of men off from others and robbing many of the means and opportunity to live rich and varied lives as befits their inclinations and potentialities. Beyond that, he appears to be saying, the demand for equality is an absurd one. Certainly his sketch is only a general picture of a classless society; were the details to be filled in it could well reveal significant differences in the influence and standing of men, the abolition of which it would be equally absurd to demand.

7/The Principle of Equality

I

From time to time we have had, in effect, to ask how far men want to take equality. We have seen, for example, that the notion of equality of influence among human beings is not one which has usually been incorporated in the demand for equality; indeed, if the notion were taken literally, it is difficult to make sense of it. What then does the demand for equality involve? Few, if any, have favoured a conception of equality which aims to make men as like each other as possible. For egalitarians in Britain the statement of the ideal which would probably command widest assent is to be found in Tawney's classic work, *Equality*. And for Tawney there was certainly no merit in striving for a society of identical human beings. His conception of equality is well expressed in these passages:

> Few men have been more acutely sensitive than Mill to the importance of encouraging the widest possible diversities of mind and taste. In arguing that 'the best state for human nature is that in which, while no one is poor, no one desires to be richer', and urging that social policy should be directed to increasing equality, he did not intend to convey that it should suppress varieties of individual genius and character, but that it was only in a society marked by a large measure of economic equality that such varieties were likely to find their full expression and due meed of appreciation.

> . . . because men are men, social institutions—property rights, and the organization of industry, and the system of public health and education—should be planned, as far as is possible, to emphasize and strengthen, not the class differences which divide, but the common humanity which unites, them.

> The more anxiously . . . a society endeavours to secure equality of consideration for all its members, the greater will be the differentiation of treatment which, when once their common human needs have been met, it accords to the special needs of different groups and individuals among them.[1]

Now there is a variety of ways to express the idea of equality and different writers tend to emphasize some forms of equality, rather than others, as of overriding importance—equality before the law, equality of basic human rights, economic equality or equality of consideration for all persons. It is not to be assumed that these are necessarily competing categories, but how is economic equality related to equality of consideration? Does the former imply absolute equality of incomes as opposed to the differential treatment of needs implied by the latter? One answer which has commonly been offered to questions such as these is that equality as a principle amounts to no more than that men should all be treated in the same way save where there is sufficient reason for treating them differently. But many have felt uneasy about this version of equality, for it seems to leave open what is to count as a sufficient reason and all kinds of invidious distinctions could make an entry that way. How then are we to formulate the principle or ideal of equality? This is a question we must tackle in stages and there is merit in starting with Aristotle whose discussion of equality is the source of some of the distinctions we still make use of today.

In Book v of the *Politics* Aristotle discusses the general causes of constitutional change, why men resort to 'sedition' (*stasis*). He says:

> At all events, whatever the aim of sedition may be, it stems in every case from inequality, though there is no inequality if unequals are treated in proportion to their mutual inequality. The desire for equality, therefore, is the mainspring of sedition. But equality is of two kinds—numerical and proportional to desert.[2]

This distinction between numerical and proportional equality enters into Aristotle's notion of distributive justice, i.e. the sort of justice that is involved in the distribution of honours or money 'or the other things that fall to be divided among those who have a share in the constitution'.[3]  Numerical equality means treating everyone in exactly the same way whereas proportional equality has regard to the relative merits of the persons concerned.[4] Hence justice requires that if two persons are equals they should have equal shares; if they are unequal they should have unequal shares, but in proportion to their inequality. The origin of quarrels and complaints, observes Aristotle, can be traced to the fact that the principle of proportional equality has been violated, as when equals have or are awarded unequal shares, or unequals equal shares. For, he says, awards should be made 'according to merit'; and, he maintains, men do commonly agree that justice in distribution involves the criterion of 'merit', though they differ as to what constitutes merit. Democrats, he tells us, tend to identify merit with the status of freemen, supporters of oligarchy with wealth or noble birth, and supporters of aristocracy with 'excellence' or 'virtue'.[5]

The principle of proportional equality, then, involves an appeal to some criterion in terms of which differential treatment is justified. It follows that if there is no significant respect in which the persons concerned are distinguishable, differential treatment would be unjustified, since equals would be treated unequally. But what is to be allowed as a significant difference such as would justify differential treatment? Aristotle is sensitive to this question and though the actual criteria he favoured would be widely criticized nowadays the *formal* requirements he laid down are incorporated in the commonly asserted principle: 'Treat people in the same manner unless there are good grounds for treating them differently', or, very briefly, 'No discrimination without sufficient reason.'

Aristotle's awareness of the problem as to what constitutes a sufficient reason for discrimination comes out clearly in this passage: 'Now justice is recognized universally as some sort of equality . . . justice involves an assignment of things to persons . . . equals are entitled to equal things. But here we are met by the important question: Equals and unequals *in what*? This is a difficult problem.'[6]

He approaches the matter on the supposition that his audience shares with him certain standards as to what is relevant. The modern reader will not, of course, go along with some of the assumptions he makes but that, given the cultural context, they hang together coherently and hence provide a *pattern of argument* which can be filled in with criteria belonging to a different set of values surely cannot be denied. In distributing the offices of state, he says, not any sort of personal quality is relevant, for unless we employ criteria appropriate to the sphere in question it could turn out that a man's height or complexion would determine his eligibility and/or suitability for political rights. (Incidentally, I take it that the English word 'complexion' could not be alternatively rendered as 'colour', which, of course, some people do regard as a relevant consideration; I know of no one who would want to insist on height as an appropriate qualification for political rights.[7]) Elaborating on this question of what is a relevant factor for differential treatment, Aristotle gives the example of the distribution of flutes among flautists:

Take a man who is a first-rate flautist, but of humble extraction and far from handsome. Blue blood and physical beauty may be greater assets than the art of flute-playing, and may excel the latter in a higher degree than our flautist excels others in his art; nevertheless, he still has a claim to the best flutes—unless the advantages of wealth and birth enhance the skill of an instrumentalist, which manifestly they do not.[8]

I have heard it said in discussion of this passage that the example given here is a bad one for the point Aristotle was wishing to make. A first-rate flautist might well get as much out of a mediocre flute as a mediocre player would get out of a good flute, and if one were distributing flutes to an orchestral group the principle of giving the best flutes to the best players would not necessarily secure the best results. But even if we were to grant this objection, the sense of Aristotle's argument is surely that 'blue-blood' and 'physical beauty' are clearly irrelevant factors in the distribution of flutes when the whole purpose of the distribution is to produce the best orchestral tone; whereas the relative skills of the instrumentalists is at least one—and probably the most—relevant factor. In the same way, Aristotle maintains, claims to political office must not be based on prowess in athletic contests; candidates for office should possess those qualities that go to make for an effective use of the office. And in Aristotle's view the relevant qualities are 'noble descent, free birth or wealth', and also 'justice and valour'. However, he goes on, if we have regard not just to the existence of the state but aim at the good life then 'education and virtue have yet stronger claims'.[9]

Hans Kelsen has criticized Aristotle's principle of proportional equality on the ground that it fails to indicate what differences among men are to be allowed as justifying discriminatory treatment. Kelsen represents the principle as follows:

If a right *a* is allotted to an individual A, and a right *b* to the individual B, the requirement of distributive justice is fulfilled if the ratio of value *a* to value *b* is equal to the ratio of value A to value B. If the individuals A and B are equal, the rights to be allotted to them must be equal too. However, there are in nature no two individuals who are really equal, since there is always a difference as to age, sex, health, wealth, and so forth.[10]

The decisive question in connection with social equality, goes on Kelsen, is what differences are relevant and Aristotle's formula provides no answer to this. 'Any privilege whatever is covered by this formula,' he asserts.[11] It would sanction special rights for persons in the higher income brackets or deny rights to persons of a certain race. Felix Oppenheim makes the same point when he says that 'every conceivable rule treats equals (in some specified respect) equally and unequals unequally'.[12]

Now the issue Kelsen raises has general application to the problem of formulating a viable principle of equality. His objection to Aristotle's principle of proportional equality, namely, that 'any privilege whatever is covered by this formula', is one that has been made, in different contexts, by many contemporary writers. Thus Sir Isaiah Berlin says of the requirement that we treat all men in the same way unless there is sufficient reason for treating them otherwise that it 'leaves open crucial issues', since it could be maintained that until 'some specific sense is given to "sufficient reason" the principle can be reduced to a trivial tautology'; and, he adds, the notion of 'sufficient reason' is suspect precisely because it 'can be made to cover almost any type of situation'.[13] J. R. Lucas argues a similar case. What he calls the principle of 'formal equality' is defined thus:

> It requires that if two people are being treated, or are to be treated, differently, there should be some relevant difference between them. Otherwise, in the absence of some differentiating feature, what is sauce for the goose is sauce for the gander, and it would be wrong to treat the two unequally, that is, not the same.

This principle, he says, commits us to very little. Given that human beings do differ from one another in all sorts of ways and that the principle, as thus formulated, contains no restriction on what is to constitute a relevant difference, the most it provides us with is 'a line of argument, but not any definite conclusion'.[14] And it is because it leaves so much open that Professor J. W. N. Watkins calls it 'the weak principle of equality', requiring no more than that 'people are to be treated equally unless some feature of their condition justifies unequal treatment'. It is equivalent, he says, to 'the formal principle of all moralities which are not actually anti-rational: "Don't act capriciously".'[15]

In the light of these criticisms it would seem beyond dispute that Aristotle's principle of proportionate equality, and the many variations thereon advanced by later writers, are open to the charge of being purely formal and hence vacuous. In itself the formula does not tell us what differences between men would render discriminatory treatment justifiable. To make the principle work at all as an instrument of social policy one would have to declare one's values, make clear what differences are to be regarded as relevant or irrelevant.

But in defence of Aristotle, though not necessarily of his particular values, it could be urged that whatever criteria one does adopt, the rules incorporating them would fall into the logical pattern of his principle of proportional equality. And since Aristotle makes plain beyond doubt the criteria which he does favour the sort of criticism Kelsen levels against him loses its force. As we have seen, the fact that a man is of free birth, of noble descent or has wealth is for him a relevant consideration in distributing political rights, as indeed it was for many of his contemporaries. And the fact that a man was a slave was considered a sufficient reason for denying him those rights. The contrast which has been drawn between the Periclean ideal and Aristotle's aristocratic leanings does not mean that the Periclean democrat would have been precluded from adopting Aristotle's principle of proportional equality. It would have been open to him to have done this while insisting that in his eyes all citizens were equals, that differences in respect of noble birth or wealth were irrelevant. The principle is in effect a kind of logical mould into which all kinds of substantial criteria can be poured. Kelsen's criticsm would be on target if it could be shown that Aristotle was unaware of the need to import criteria for differentiation into his formula as a condition of its doing a substantive job. But he *was* aware of this. To quote him again. 'Equals are entitled to equal things, but the important question is: equals and unequals *in what?*'

II

The problem which emerges from our brief survey of Aristotle's views on equality is how to frame a principle or theory of equality which though it has to be couched in general terms yet escapes the charge of being merely formal or vacuous and hence in danger of justifying 'any privilege whatever'. It will be necessary to go again over some of the ground covered in the first section of this chapter, but I propose to begin by considering what is regarded as the most extreme version of the principle of equality that it is possible to hold, a version that has probably not been adopted by any political theorist of note but which Felix Oppenheim says was championed by some nineteenth-century anarchists.[16]

This is the principle of 'equal treatment of all in every respect' or the 'strong principle of unconditional equality', as Watkins puts it, '[which] says that people are to be treated equally whatever their condition'.[17]

It is important to notice that this is not the same as asserting that 'every human being is equally deserving of respect' or that 'every person has the right to equality ofconsideration', since these formulae are commonly held by those who advance them to be quite compatible with various kinds of differential treatment, which the former seems unequivocally to rule out. The principle of unconditional equality, as Watkins argues, would require that (assuming non-siege conditions) 'everybody should be treated exactly alike, irrespective of whether they are competent, married, old lags, youths, alcoholics or whatever'; and this, he contends, is 'palpably absurd'.[18]

Now although Oppenheim states that the principle of 'equal treatment of all in every respect' was advocated by some nineteenth-century anarchists the nearest position to this of which I know was the one taken up in the 'Manifesto of the Equals', to which I have already referred. Denying the claim that 'absolute equality is but a chimera' and rejecting the suggestion that men should be satisfied with 'equality of rights', the Manifesto goes on:

> We declare that we can no longer suffer that the great majority of men shall labour and sweat to serve and pamper the extreme minority . . . Let there be at length an end to this enormous scandal, which posterity will scarcely credit. Away for ever with the revolting distinctions of rich and poor, of great and little, of masters and servants, of *governors* and *governed*. Let there be no longer any other differences in mankind than those of age and sex. Since all have the same wants, and the same faculties, let all have accordingly the same education—the same nourishment. They are content with one sun, and the same air for all; why should not the like portion, and the same quality of food, suffice for each according to his wants?[19]

What should make one hesitate to describe this as a call for 'equal treatment of all in every respect' is that age and sex are allowed as relevant differentiating factors for the way people are to be treated, that although in one place it proposes 'the same nourishment' for all there is nevertheless the recognition that food should be distributed to each 'according to his wants' (which I take to be a way of saying that a heavy industrial worker, for instance, is entitled to more, or different, food from a sedentary clerk and that the needs of an invalid are different from those of the strong and healthy), and that the abolition of the 'revolting distinctions' which are specifically mentioned fall a good

4

deal short of the absolute equality that would literally treat everyone in the same way in *every respect*.

However, regardless of the fact that no one may have actually aspired to a society in which all persons are treated equally in every respect, the attempt to conceive such a society faces a number of formidable obstacles, so much so that it must lead one to wonder if it really is a coherent notion. But it may be worth examining the idea if only for the guidance it can give us in the elaboration of a viable conception of equality.[20]

Part of the difficulty is whether to construe the formula in an absolute and literal sense, for if one tries to interpret it in this manner it seems to postulate as an ideal situation one in which we should virtually cease to exist as recognizable human beings. Even if we assume that we could all be engineered into a uniform set of living creatures there would still be obstacles to providing strict equality of treatment. Inanimate physical objects cannot all be located in the same place at the same time and it makes no sense to suppose it could matter to *them*, though it could to *us*. It makes no difference how a set of identical marbles is arranged in a bag, but it does matter to human beings as to where they are placed, where they live and work—that is, quite apart from the nature of their work. For example, being born and brought up in an environment with *relatively* clean air can make a difference to one's health and happiness and this promises to be an increasingly important, rather than a fading, problem. Similarly if one lives within earshot of an airport or a motorway or superhighway. Of course the goal of ensuring for everyone a healthy and pleasant environment is a worthy one and it may turn out that we shall eventually be able to take great strides in that direction. Even so, could *everyone* be equally well or ill placed with regard to the various sources of enjoyment and distress—e.g. access to beaches, the countryside, art galleries, first class orchestras, first-division football grounds, major league baseball stadiums, and the national theatre or, on the debit side, proximity to the many and mounting sources of annoyance and frustration in our surroundings?

At which point I can hear the complaint that the whole thing is being reduced to absurdity. Well, where does one have to stop in the search for equality of treatment for *all* persons in *every* respect? It might also be said that we are not, and are not likely ever to be, *equally* interested in access to, or freedom from, the 'pains and pleasures' mentioned above. Yet it would surely be part of this version of the egalitarian ideal that we should all become more and more the same in the things we like and dislike. Were this not so diversity in abilities, tastes, and interests would constitute a breeding ground of inequality in the shape, among other ways, of the different impact made on us in our upbringing and education by those on whom our growth and development depend. And here we face a crucial question that any would-be advocate of this form of equality must face: namely, equality of opportunity. For if we are all to be treated in the same way this must carry with it no more important requirement than that none of us should be better or worse off in the upbringing and education we receive than anyone else, which, as has often been argued, is an unattainable ideal for human beings of anything like the sort we now are and seem likely for a long time to be.

A good example of this line of argument is John Charvet's discussion of equality of opportunity.[21] He claims that there cannot be a satisfactory formulation of the principle of equality of opportunity since the notion is itself incoherent, 'for a complete formulation of it renders it incompatible with any form of human society'.[22] He develops his case in relation to equality of opportunity in education which, he maintains, does not start in the schools and hence requires uniform treatment in families —an evident impossibility. To remedy this all children might be brought up in state nurseries, but to achieve their purpose the nurseries would have to be run on vigorously uniform lines. Could we guarantee equal treatment of the young even in these circumstances? There are two possibilities, he says: either (i) 'that all those through associating with whom individuals develop themselves, should be equal in their capacities to help such development', or (ii) 'that there should be no such association at all'. Both of which, he asserts, are 'absurd fantasies'.[23] So he concludes that equality of opportunity is an incoherent notion because it requires of the growing person's relations with others that they either be literally the same as everyone else's, a provision which it is impossible to secure, or that there should be no dependence on others at all, i.e. no human society. But Charvet does not deny that in, say, the control of entrance into the civil service or higher education some version of the principle of equality would be applicable. Indeed he suggests that our old friend 'the formal principle of equality—that equals should be treated equally' is appropriate here since we could invoke it to rule out certain factors, such as class or wealth, which we may hold to be irrelevant to entry in these spheres.[24]

A radical egalitarian who recognized the absurdity of trying to secure equality of treatment in every respect but still wanted to insist on the relevance of the idea of equality of opportunity might begin by pointing to the barriers created by class, education, and wealth to the fulfilment of capacities which, he would claim, there is every reason to suppose are far more widely spread among the population than our present restrictive arrangements induce many of us to believe. This was certainly Tawney's view. More recent expositions of this type of argument have had the advantage of the results of detailed research into the relationship between, for example, social class and educational achievement. I do not propose to look at those details here, but a paper based on familiarity with some of these results, which approaches the idea of equality of opportunity in a less hostile mood than Charvet's is Professor Bernard Williams' well-known essay, 'The Idea of Equality'.[25] And interestingly enough there is at least this measure of agreement between Charvet and Williams, despite their deep-seated differences: namely a common recognition of the profound consequences for social life of an *attempt* to secure equality of opportunity in its full sense.

Williams defines equality of opportunity in terms of access to certain goods and he distinguishes three such categories, one of which covers goods that not everyone can have even if they want them. In the latter group there are goods such as being in a position of authority, being in control or being esteemed which, as he says, 'are *by their very nature* limited'.[26] But another sort of goods in this group could be made more widely available through appropriate social reforms; university education, he suggests, falls into this category. Similarly, that wealth is still a means of securing a privileged kind of secondary education is open to social remedy, as is also the continuing advantage of wealth in gaining access to litigation. So 'imaginative social reform' can do much to change the environmental factors that stand in the way of equal access to certain goods, and education is the principal example he uses to develop his argument.[27] Short of social reform, he contends, equality of opportunity is not really being assured for two groups of persons, one of which benefits from social circumstances while the other is handicapped by an adverse social environment. Equality of opportunity requires that the circumstances of the latter be improved or, more realistically, that in the future everyone should benefit from favourable social circumstances.

It is here, I think, that Charvet and Williams are at odds, the latter appearing to hold that what is now adverse in the environment for some persons is to a substantial degree 'curable', the former firmly of the view that the many and important differences in upbringing which affect, say, educational potential, are inevitable in any society. What is at issue between them could I suspect be resolved, if at all, only by a more careful and detailed enquiry into the ways that diverse family circumstances—apart from such things as housing and wealth, which are indeed 'curable'—make a difference to a growing person's 'potential'. And even if some elements in that situation were agreed to be 'curable' the question of 'cost' would arise, for some people would be likely to shrink from using the kind of state interference necessary to effect a remedy because other values stood higher in their scale than a desire to secure strict equality of opportunity.

In fairness to Williams it would be wrong to represent him as a fanatical and thorough-going advocate of equality of opportunity, regardless of 'cost', for one of the most interesting parts of his paper follows on from the point when he asks how far one should move in changing the social environment in order to secure greater equality of opportunity. As he puts it:

> Where should this stop? Should it even stop at the boundaries of heredity? Suppose it were discovered that when all curable environmental disadvantages had been dealt with, there was a residual genetic difference in brain constitution, for instance, which was correlated with differences in desired types of ability; but that the brain constitution could in fact be changed by an operation.[28]

In a footnote he refers to the possibility—confidently predicted by some writers in the years since the essay was published—of producing individual qualities to order by what has come to be called 'genetic engineering', a prospect which he regards as having 'dizzying consequences'. However, the state of affairs imagined in the passage I have quoted is admitted to be a fantasy, but it would, says Williams, be a condition in which 'the individuals would be regarded as in all respects equal in themselves . . . [and] in these circumstances, where everything about a person is controllable, equality of opportunity and absolute equality seem to coincide . . .'[29] Now, in saying this, Williams seems to me to come close to Charvet's position, for if it is a condition of achieving equality of opportunity that we have to enter into a 'fantasy world' of the sort he has portrayed, the implication is that social life as we understand it, even when remedied by radical improvements in the environment, is not compatible with the requirements of the principle of equality of opportunity.

At this point one is inclined to ask whether it really matters that some persons are more able or single-minded than others, that some, rather than others, should have the qualities that make for 'success'

in our competitive and status-conscious society. The very fact that
'genetic engineering' should be envisaged at all as a possible remedy for
inequality of opportunity suggests such a strong desire to ensure uniform treatment for all persons as to exclude or belittle other values and
indeed to ignore certain aspects of equality itself.[30] For as Williams
recognizes, there is in the complex of ideas that go to make up equality
a commitment to respect other human beings irrespective of their
abilities and achievements. After all, the rights which the U.N. Declaration assigns to all men equally are not thought to be dependent on their
being possessed of a certain level of intelligence, prowess in the arts or
sport, or a position of authority in industry or government, any more
than they are dependent on one's racial origins or religious beliefs. Of
course, if social arrangements make the effective exercise of these rights
impossible then there is an urgent case for changing them. In this sense
inequalities of opportunity must demand our attention and call for
remedy. But no man has a right to a high I.Q. any more than he has a
right to be esteemed. Those engaged in the zealous search for total
equality of opportunity have really fallen into using the language which
stems from seeing life as a race and thereby they have conceded to the
ethics of competition and the love of prowess something that ought not
to be conceded by anyone who conceives of equality as a humane ideal.
Tawney showed great wisdom in these matters and expressed it well
when he said:

> . . . the truth [is] that it is absurd and degrading for men to make
> much of their intellectual and moral superiority to each other,
> and still more of their superiority in the arts which bring wealth
> and power, because, judged by their place in any universal
> scheme, they are all infinitely great or infinitely small . . . It does
> not follow [from the fact that some men are inferior to others in
> respect of their intellectual endowments] that such individuals
> or classes should receive less consideration than others, or should
> be treated as inferior in respect of such matters as legal status,
> or health, or economic arrangements, which are within the control
> of the community.'[31]

The uproar which followed Professor Arthur Jensen's reported
findings on the lower average I.Q. of American Blacks, in relation to
American Whites, and his contention that this inferiority could not be
wholly attributed to environmental factors, provides an example of the
sort of inference people are often led to draw from certain alleged facts

about human qualities. I am not competent to pass judgement on the reliability of the assumptions and methods used in Jensen's research, nor do I want to enter the controversy as to whether he should have launched his enquiry at all, but the implications for social policy that some of his critics have seen in the results seem to me to be typical of the kind of thinking Tawney was arguing against. Among those who have attacked Jensen are some who appear to believe that, were his results well-founded, they would somehow constitute a justification for the various forms of discrimination suffered by American Blacks; and this is about as valid an inference to draw as would be an attempt to justify Nazi policy toward the Jews because of the latter's higher average intelligence in relation to pure Aryans.

It may well be true, as a social psychologist from Cambridge is reported to have said, that 'test constructors are middle-class white academics and, not surprisingly, the test items represent their values . . . [that] the only valid scientific claim is that, on average, black children, working class children, Eskimos, West Indians and so on are less good at answering questions designed for white middle-class children'.[32] But even if we were to be satisfied with the scientific validity of Jensen's claims, what would follow? It is beyond question, for instance, that American Blacks have dominated the history of jazz, a form of music for which some of us have a particular fondness; yet I would hesitate to conclude, on that account alone, that they were entitled to special privileges in, say, university entrance, housing, athletics, or courts of law. In a radio talk on this controversy Max Hammerton concluded that the differences which Jensen claims to have discovered *could* be genetically determined, that the results were 'strongly suggestive' rather than firmly established and that 'reasonable doubt still remains'. But, he went on to ask, what if they were put beyond reasonable doubt, should that induce us to change our attitude to racial oppression? Not at all, 'racism would remain precisely as repugnant as before'; an affirmation of his moral outlook which he supports with an appeal to David Hume's famous remarks about the logical gulf between factual premises and moral conclusions—remarks whose interpretation, in this context at any rate, it would be niggling and pedantic to quarrel over.[33] Like Hammerton, confronted with the information that an identifiable social group has a lower than average I.Q. (leaving aside the difficulties raised about this concept) or most of whose members would never be able to make much of Russell's theory of descriptions, I would be bound to ask, 'Well, does that mean they are not entitled for instance to proper benefits in sickness and old age, to a fair trial, to decent housing and to the best education they and their children can derive advantage from—and in all these and other respects to be treated on a par with the whites?'

What may appear as a digression from the main theme of the argument does, however, have a bearing on the principle of absolute or unconditional equality (i.e. equal treatment of all in every respect), and its related principle, equality of opportunity. The former requires either that, despite the fact of human diversity, we should all be treated in the same way in all respects or that we should move toward a society in which individuals would be uniformly alike. In such a society the principle of treating equals equally would have universal application and the awkward problem of meting out identical treatment to individuals with varying abilities, needs and tastes would not arise. But, as we have seen, a society of literally uniform individuals is hard to imagine. Would we, for example, all be equally healthy? For it would be generally admitted that the fact of a man's being ill is a good reason for his receiving medical attention and no egalitarian—or anyone else—has ever argued that differential treatment in cases of this kind is impermissible. What, however, of a man's outstanding talent for the piano? But to allow special aptitudes such as this to flourish is to violate absolute equality. As opposed to the welcome given by Tawney and most contemporary egalitarians to the diversity of talents the principle cannot accommodate itself to them, as though they were an evil to be avoided.

Yet may it not be that there is a curious form of logic underlying the absolute equality idea, which would run something like this? The existence of a significant difference between persons is commonly taken as a sufficient reason for discriminatory treatment, but there can be no watertight definition of a 'sufficient reason'; hence all kinds of inequalities can be justified once we depart from the principle of strict equality. The latter therefore cannot work smoothly so long as there is diversity among men, so if equality is to mean anything we must create a society where the principle will operate without producing blatant anomalies and thus inducing a sense of injustice. For justice consists in treating equals equally.[34] What imparts a kind of sense to this line of argument is adoption of the view that to justify equality of treatment there must be equality in the attributes of the persons concerned, otherwise the move from factual premises to moral principle is unwarranted. But, as we saw when discussing Aristotle, not all differences have to count. There is nothing illogical about giving the vote or a fair trial to all adults even though they differ enormously in their capacities for playing chess, climbing the Eiger and speaking on public platforms.

Because of the absurdity involved in any attempt to apply absolute
equality to men as we now know them, and the nightmarish quality of
the society it would be necessary to create for it to be viable, some
writers have been led to wonder whether equality as such has any value,
though others merely argue that as a principle of treatment it must
never be paramount. An example of the former is Professor H. J.
McCloskey. He says that though equality, either in the shape of the
principle of equal treatment of all in all respects or as an ideal condition
of society in which we would all be uniformly alike, has never been
explicitly advocated by any serious thinker, some contemporary egalitarians appear to him to aspire to 'a society in which our abilities, tastes,
conditions, etc., are as like as they can be'.[35] The ethos of suburbia,
'with its stress on uniformity and conformity', seems to McCloskey
to come near to adopting an equality of this sort as a goal. But, he
maintains, the usual demand for equality is aimed at removing *unjustifiable* inequalities and the logic of this demand implies that not all
inequalities are evil and hence that equality as such cannot be a worthy
end. He goes on:

> A state which concerns itself solely with liberty, or with the
> general happiness, or with justice, is one which does not com-
> mend itself to most of us. However, there is a big difference
> between such states and one geared to equality. In the cases of
> the former we feel that a good is being realized but at the
> expense of many other goods. In the case of equality (which,
> as we have seen, involves unjustly treating dissimilars similarly,
> or making people similar, or levelling out all differences, personal
> and other, to achieve a dull uniformity and conformity), there
> is no evident good of any sort being realized through or in the
> equality itself, that what good such a state achieved would be
> due to equality coinciding with some other good such as justice,
> liberty, fraternity, happiness. In any case, the demand for
> equality seems more likely to collide rather than to coincide
> with the demands for these other goods.[36]

That equality often conflicts with other values is part of the
reason why many writers cannot accept it as a paramount goal. British
political theory in the twentieth century has commonly postulated the
development of the capacities of all men in their richest diversity as
the ultimate end of social policy and egalitarians such as Tawney fall
clearly into this tradition. Of course it is a tradition within which some

particular thinkers have put more emphasis on, say, reducing inequalities in the distribution of wealth or in educational opportunity than others, but they unite in their commitment to individual variety rather than mass conformity, to encouragement of individual creative talents rather than uniformity and achievement. And as Mill so cogently argued, liberty is a condition of individual development as well as part of its meaning. Now liberty in this sense cannot flourish in conditions of absolute equality. This is not to say that equality should always give way to liberty; it is rather to urge that both equality and liberty are necessary elements in the conception of a humane society. To the extent that absolute equality is accorded the highest priority so we reject the idea that human fulfilment demands a variety of responses to the highly diverse aspirations of the human character.

We seem to emerge then with little respect for absolute equality, but is that the end of the matter? May there not be some sense in which men should all be treated in the same way, perhaps not in *all respects* but at least in some? For example, it has often been said that the essential and important ingredient in all demands for equality is 'equality of consideration'. This notion of equality of consideration has been elucidated in a variety of ways and I shall take Rashdall's version as a convenient starting-point; more recent versions fall into the same general structure.

Rashdall advances the principle that 'every human being is of equal intrinsic value, and is therefore entitled to equal respect' as an 'exacter expression of the Christian ideal of Brotherhood'. He goes on, however, to point out that the principle does not require that every person be given an equal share of wealth or of political power but rather 'equal consideration in the distribution of ultimate good'.[37] He takes it to be self-evident, to be an 'analytical judgement', to say that what is recognized as being of value in one person must be recognized as being of the same value in another, 'provided it is really the same thing that is implied in the assertion that it has value'.[38] Such axioms, he agrees, cannot of themselves solve practical moral problems—they are 'purely formal'—but they do offer guidelines on how to distribute 'the good' once its nature is known. What is implied by the principle of equal respect for all persons is impartiality in the treatment of all men; it rules out inequality, 'or rather arbitrary inequality—inequality not justified by the requirements of social well-being, or some other general and rational principle—in the treatment of individuals'. No man, he asserts, has a right to anything unconditionally except the right to be equally considered. The rights of man are all 'ultimately resolvable into the one supreme and unconditional right—*the right to considera-tion*'.[39]

Now it is important to notice that the respect in which all men are to be treated equally, namely that they all have the right to equal con-sideration, is not construed so as to exclude inequality of treatment in other respects, e.g. in the distribution of certain goods. And this looks as if we are being thrown back on to the principle of conditional equality, i.e. all persons to be treated in the same way unless there are sufficient reasons for treating particular persons or groups differently. This comes out clearly in E. F. Carritt's account. Like Rashdall, Carritt takes equality of consideration to be man's basic right and for him this means, among other things, that every man has the right to life and to liberty; but the fundamental right is to have his claims equally con-sidered, to equality of treatment *in like situations*: 'men not only have the right to have their claims equally considered, but equal claims to benefit, improvement, and non-interference until some stronger claim to the contrary has been established'. Hence 'the burden of proof lies with those who desire inequality'. Carritt's formula therefore is ex-pressed thus: 'equal treatment of those who are equal in relevant respects'. What would justify differential treatment? What is to be counted as 'relevant' here? Carritt's answer, very briefly, is that we should take into consideration only 'morally relevant circumstances'; for 'equality of consideration means impartiality . . . the effort to dis-count private preferences . . . and this implies that where we see no moral ground for differentiation they should be treated alike'. And examples of what he would accept as morally relevant grounds, indeed the main ones, are 'need', 'capacity' and 'desert'.[40]

Although there are important differences, especially as to the area of mankind whose claims are to be equally considered, the similarity in logical form between the accounts of equality of consideration given by Rashdall and Carritt on the one hand and Aristotle's principle of pro-portionate equality on the other cannot but have struck the reader very forcibly. It is because absolute or unconditional equality has not pro-vided us with an acceptable principle that we have to return to Aristotle's or the modern variations thereon, bearing particularly in mind the point that whereas it allows the variety of treatment of persons which justice seems to call for it has also been charged with affording cover for 'any privilege whatever'. But first let us go back for a moment to the question we raised earlier about the respect, or respects, in which it could be said that men should be treated equally. I said then that, given the absurdity of absolute equality, there may yet be a sense in which we should wish to assert that *all* men should be treated in 'the same way'. One possibility has been indicated, namely 'equality of consideration'. Other possibilities include 'equality of satisfaction of basic needs', 'equality in the possession of natural (human) rights' and 'equality of respect for all men'. These notions share a good deal of common ground but there are also interesting differences among them, although I do not wish to take up that question here. What does need emphasis in this context is that none of these formulae rule out differential treatment, so they all have an important similarity with the principle we are now to examine more closely.

III

Conditional equality or, as some have called it, the *weak* principle of equality, prescribes that all persons should be treated equally (in the same way) save when there are reasons for treating them differently. It is called 'weak' because as such it contains no instructions as to what is to count as 'reasons'. It corresponds to Professor Ch. Perelman's notion of 'formal' or 'abstract' justice. People may be treated according to their merits or their needs, he says, and it is just to treat them in the same way if, in respect of their merits or needs, they are equal. The feature by virtue of which they are judged to be equal or unequal he calls 'essential' and the definition of formal justice he offers runs like this: formal justice is 'a principle of action in accordance with which beings of one and the same essential category must be treated in the same way'. It is 'formal' justice, he says, because the definition is 'a purely formal idea . . . [it] tells us neither when two beings participate in an essential category nor how they ought to be treated'.[41] In other words the principle does not, in itself, provide an answer to Aristotle's question, 'equals and unequals *in what?*'

The very fact that it is 'a purely formal idea' can be regarded, from different aspects, as both an advantage and a disadvantage. In its favour can be cited its success in avoiding the obvious injustices that would result from treating persons with different needs in the same way. It sanctions special provision for, say, the blind pupil as against those with normal vision, and extra rations in wartime for coalminers and expectant mothers. On the other hand it says nothing to rule out discrimination on racial or religious grounds. Moreover, it is silent on the vital question of what is proper treatment, i.e. the sort of treatment men are to be given. For instance, free access to a wide variety of newspapers and journals could be denied equally to us all or we may equally have to undergo indoctrination in the thoughts of a great leader; equality of treatment in such circumstances would not be taken universally as a value to be prized.

How then to strengthen the principle of conditional equality? Put in its bare form it seems to amount to no more than: 'no discrimination without a reason'. We often come across the requirement that the reasons must be 'relevant' and/or 'sufficient'. But can this serve our purpose: will not discriminators take to be 'relevant and sufficient' reasons which could well permit forms of discrimination that 'humane and rational persons' would wish to exclude? The oft-levelled criticisms of conditional equality seem therefore to be well-based. Its purely formal character, though making it more resilient than absolute equality, renders it 'compatible with any substantive principle of distribution',[42] consistent with 'any privilege (or burden) whatever'. Thus in our search for a viable version of equality we seem, for the moment, to be at a dead end. Let us change direction a little.

In respect of those matters which are likely to give rise to charges of unfair discrimination the injunctions 'Do not discriminate without a reason' or 'Do not discriminate without a relevant and sufficient reason' seem almost superfluous. If I walk down a busy street and glance only at some of the passers-by my conduct will not provoke charges of discrimination. Would we even talk of it as discrimination or differential treatment? However we describe it, people are not going to assess it in relation to some idea of equality; though one cannot say that in some very special circumstances it would not give cause for complaint. Historically speaking, the idea of equality has been typically invoked, directly or by implication, when men are protesting against what they see as injustices, unfair discrimination or unjustified persecution of particular minority groups; and the protests have arisen because of the treatment accorded to Armenians, Jews, Blacks, and homosexuals; over the franchise, the maldistribution of wealth, the uneven burden of taxation, or unequal opportunities in education. We might say that issues such as these are the contexts of applicability for equality and that outside them it would be absurd to invoke the idea. Now in these and similar contexts the discriminators have had reasons for differential treatment and reasons which were, for them, sufficient. Indeed it might even be said that in these contexts the formula of conditional equality is a description rather than—or at least as much as—a prescriptive principle. To throw the principle at the discriminators in this sort of

context would be an idle gesture; for the discrimination complained of is a matter of deliberate social policy, introduced or maintained by men who have reasons for what they are doing and in whose eyes these reasons constitute a justification.

This point is not without importance in connection with the quest for a justification of equality, for if the principle under consideration is left open—as indeed the wording of the formula does leave it open—as to what counts as 'a reason' or 'a sufficient reason' for discrimination the demand or request for justification of the principle seems odd, since giving reasons for differential treatment is a common procedure, part of what is meant by rational discourse. It is the nature of the reasons themselves rather than a failure to have or to give them which is usually at issue: the Nazis had and gave reasons for persecuting the Jews, just as do the Soviet authorities for their treatment of Solzhenitsyn and other dissident intellectuals. If it were a question of discrimination for which no reasons were advanced then we could put up a case for having them disclosed along lines similar to those involved in the principle of the accountability of office holders or the idea of responsible government.

Of course in matters of 'private concern' such a demand would be inappropriate since it would often so intrude into the area of personal choice as to constitute an invasion of privacy. A man's choice of his friends is a different matter from an employer's discretion in the hiring of labour or a law distributing the franchise. Where we draw the line between personal freedom to discriminate without obligation to declare one's reasons and the requirement of public accountability in matters of public concern might in some cases be 'arbitrary'; but the decision as to whether or not the call for reasons is legitimate would still be one for which a case could be made. Professor D. D. Raphael argues that the requirement of impartiality or non-discrimination applies only to those 'holding an office or role of authority or guardianship'.[43] This suggestion may perhaps not coincide exactly with what I have in mind as the 'area of accountability' in respect of giving reasons for discrimination, and there may be disagreements over what constitutes 'an office or role of authority', but it does provide a useful indication that some sort of viable distinction can be established and that is all that is required just here.

If I may pursue this question of having reasons for discrimination a little further, it would not I think be too fanciful to liken the requirement which the principle of conditional equality makes—especially in view of the area we are mainly concerned with, i.e. matters of *deliberate* social policy—to the requirement that there should be evidence to support factual assertions. There is of course at least one important difference between the two cases, namely that the reasons are usually either explicitly specified or are implicit in the policy involving discriminatory treatment, whereas evidence in support of factual assertions is often not adduced at all at the time the assertions are made—though the person making the assertion is committed to recognizing that it should be supplied were his statement to be challenged. But there is at least this in common between them: the request for a justification of the requirements, as if we had to show why 'reasons' and 'evidence' were legitimate things to ask for, makes about as much sense in either case.

Clearly I do not intend to include among factual assertions such statements as 'I have a toothache' or 'I dreamt about Lenin last night'. The assertions I have in mind are mainly exemplified by the publicly verifiable statements that we find in the sciences, history, and legal proceedings. My contention is simply that should anyone wish to deny that factual assertions, when challenged, need to be backed up by evidence he cannot understand what is involved in making a factual assertion. We could try to show him the connection between statements of fact and supporting evidence, but would what we might do in the way of pointing this out be a *justification* of the requirement that factual assertions be backed by evidence? Similarly if someone did not see how differential treatment is related to the reasons for it, would anything said by way of explanation amount to a *justification* of the principle, 'Do not discriminate without a reason'? Having, and in appropriate cases giving, reasons for differential treatment, I am saying, is as much part of rational conduct as having, and giving, evidence for factual statements. They are so bound up with modes of thought characteristic of our way of life that anyone who wished to suggest that they are open to adoption or rejection—as we might abandon sherry or a cocktail for whisky before dinner or introduce a system of decimal coinage or metric measurement—cannot really appreciate what would be involved in trying to do without them. It is considerations of this kind, I take it, that lie behind Rashdall's remark that the principle of equity, 'one man's good is of as much intrinsic worth as the like good of another', has the form of 'a merely analytical judgement', in which respect, he says, it resembles an axiom in mathematics.[44]

My purpose in dwelling on the relationship between 'reasons' and 'differential treatment' is chiefly to draw attention to some necessary distinctions which have to be made if we are to attach sense to the idea of justifying equality; for clearly the prior question is, what exactly are

we being invited to justify? If we are being asked to make out a case
for the practice of giving reasons in support of differential treatment
the response must be quite different from that to a request for a defence
of the particular reasons we may advance as legitimate criteria for discrimination. Writers who have discussed the problem of justifying
equality do not always recognize the importance of this distinction.
When we see it argued that equality is an ultimate value, something
self-evident, incapable of being itself justified, we should determine
just what it is that is being put in this category and the sense in which
it is self-evident or ultimate. If we do that it may turn out that the
question of justification, as we normally speak of justification, simply
does not arise. I shall return to this problem again, later.

One way of trying to prevent the principle of conditional equality
from yielding unwelcome results is to insist that the meaning or force
of 'reasons' is such as to rule out what would be regarded as objectionable grounds for discrimination. We might try to make the term 'reasons'
bear the whole weight of this task or, alternatively, put the weight on a
prefix such as 'relevant' or 'sufficient'.

An example of a writer who, in a different context from ours, wants
to assign a force to 'reasons' which would have the result of excluding
at least some of the undesirable grounds advanced in support of discrimination is Professor Richard Flathman in his book, *The Public
Interest*. Flathman contrasts decisions supported by reasons with
arbitrary decisions. To give reasons, he says, is to advance grounds, in
the shape of 'facts or circumstances', in support of our actions and
beliefs; but it is also 'to engage in the art of reasoning . . . to think in a
connected, sensible, or logical manner' as opposed to an 'irrational,
absurd or ridiculous' manner; and this implies the rejection of 'I want'
as a reason for a decision as opposed to 'I want because . . .'[45] He adds:
'Although general, these requirements are not vacuous. To require
that the grounds of a decision meet the canons of reason is to require
something which we all understand and without which we could not
live together.'[46] Flathman is concerned, among other things, to show
both that the concept of 'reasons' imposes limits on what can be adduced
in support of a decision if they are to qualify as 'reasons' and is yet wide
enough to escape the Humean charge that 'reason' is ineffective, or at
least has a very restricted role, in moral argument because, for Hume,
'reason' is identified with strictly deductive procedures. Consequently,
if we take 'reasons' in this sense, Flathman argues, two persons may
disagree and advance different supporting reasons for their respective
positions without necessarily having to regard each other's reasons as

absurd or ridiculous. Reasoning in this manner is preferable to relying on 'I want' or 'I like'; it minimizes the element of whim and caprice.

Apart from certain difficulties internal to Flathman's view, it may be doubted whether it would succeed in eliminating as 'reasons' the grounds for discrimination that egalitarians principally have in mind. Would, for example, the grounds advanced by the Nazis for their treatment of the Jews fail to qualify as 'reasons' on Flathman's test?[47] Or the case put up by certain theologians in the Dutch Reformed Church for apartheid? I doubt it. We might wish to say that the reasons advanced are bad ones, but that is a different line of criticism. We might even want to argue that the 'official' reasons put out are just a smokescreen designed to cover up, or provide a gloss on, the 'real reasons' which are basically ones of personal advantage, group privilege and simple racial prejudice. But even if the latter were a correct account of the position, the fact that a particular group would stand to lose its privileges from, say, the enfranchisement of the South African Blacks would still be a reason for its policy—not necessarily a worthy reason, but still a reason, and I see nothing in Flathman's account of 'reasons' that would be sufficient to rule it out of court. For as we have noticed already, the unpleasant truth is that the various forms of discrimination to which enlightened persons have objected have, to my knowledge, invariably been accompanied by some doctrine or theory that seeks to justify the discrimination and in terms of the purely formal character of the conditional equality principle they have satisfied its requirements. Discriminators, to repeat, have their reasons; it is the moral—or immoral—quality of the reasons which give rise to criticism, and moral criticism has to go beyond the point where Flathman's analysis leaves off. But there are one or two aspects of his analysis I want to look at before moving on to this vital question of the moral character of the reasons for discrimination; for that they must be moral before they can be held to justify unequal treatment is a contention put forward by several writers which must be taken very seriously.

Flathman seems to suggest that 'I want' and 'I like' can only be reasons for arbitrary decisions and I am sure that many examples could be cited to support this view. But there are areas of conduct in which there can be no question of being under an obligation to answer to others if one's actions are capricious and arbitrary. Our concern is with equality as a principle of *public policy* and in this field it is certainly true that arbitrariness on the part of decision makers and administrators has a significance which it does not normally assume in personal matters. Raphael's point about impartiality being a requirement for those who hold offices or have roles of authority would enter into the distinction we are trying to make here.

One is not, however, accountable for the discrimination exercised in the choice of one's friends or for the fact that one frequents this rather than that supermarket. I doubt whether 'arbitrary' or 'capricious' are the appropriate terms to use of this kind of behaviour; and if they were then caprice and arbitrariness are perfectly in order. Moreover, what would it be like to be impartial in the making of friends? If I propose going on holiday in the Oetztal and want a climbing companion surely the fact of my liking or not liking a person is a highly relevant consideration in deciding whether to invite him along? Maybe one of the possible candidates who is the most skilled on rock and ice happens to be a person I do not like and I then have to balance up the advantages of having an expert partner against his disadvantages as a companion. In mountaineering of an entirely different order, how people get on with one another, whether they like each other, can turn the scales in the direction of success or failure for the whole expedition. The leader of the expedition (an office or role of authority?) has a duty to take the mutual likes and dislikes of his potential team (including his own) into account.[48] But whereas 'I like' is an appropriate and relevant factor in this context it is certainly not in the business of awarding examination marks, for it would be commonly agreed that the criteria for academic grading have to do with the nature of the activity to be assessed, i.e. scholarly achievement. Liking or not liking a student are therefore irrelevant to the teacher's task. In the same way the criteria for judging whether someone was a great batsman have to do with the aims and standards of cricket. To say that Gary Sobers, for example, is not a great batsman because of the colour of his skin is to bring in an absurd and irrelevant criterion. Now, could we say that discrimination in matters of social and political policy, in the distribution of rights and duties, has as a context certain standards and purposes which set limits to what can be a proper, as opposed to an irrelevant and absurd, criterion for discrimination?

In the early part of the *Republic* Socrates argues that there is an analogy between ruling and medicine such that the duties which a doctor has toward his patients are paralleled by duties which a ruler has toward his subjects. Neither doctor nor ruler, if each is to be true to his role, can regard his task as solely one of self-advancement. Now if there were generally accepted standards of this sort by which we could judge the performance of rulers and assess the worth of institutions and laws they would clearly constitute an important part of the set of values we should need to have for deciding on the legitimacy of various forms of differential treatment. Yet declarations of general principles, if they are to gain widespread acceptance, have to be so loosely worded that they are open to divergent interpretations and thus leave 'rational men' to disagree over their application to specific issues. Thus while those subscribing to such a general declaration would be unanimous in rejecting, say, the colour of a man's hair as a criterion for distributing the franchise there would be many important matters over which men disagreed and no party could claim a monopoly of 'reason' or the exclusive right to interpret the clauses of the declaration. So quite apart from the possibility that even the most generally formulated scheme of values might be repudiated by persons who think in 'a connected, sensible or logical manner' and who would be prepared to 'give reasons' for their decisions, acceptance of the scheme itself is no guarantee that we shall agree on the interpretation to be put on the criteria for legitimate discrimination in particular cases. And to be fair, Flathman does not imply or even set out to show that a common commitment to the practice of 'giving reasons' (in his sense) will automatically yield an acceptable set of criteria which would operate without dissension in all cases. His argument is aimed mainly at those fields in which the requirement to give reasons does operate to reduce the dangers of caprice and arbitrariness, i.e. courts, tribunals and the quasi-judicial activities of administrative officials, whose decisions should indeed be impartial rather than the expression of likes and dislikes. But the decisions of these bodies are made within the context of laws; and laws may discriminate for bad reasons. And the fact that laws can be unjust is not attributable to the failure of the legislators to have and give reasons.

The suggestion I now want to take up is that the grounds or reasons specified in the conditional equality principle are to be understood as reasons which constitute a justification of differential treatment in a morally relevant way. Carritt, we saw, takes equality of consideration to mean, among other things, 'impartiality' and 'consideration only of morally relevant circumstances'. Men, he says, should be treated alike when there is 'no moral ground for differentiation'.[49] And Raphael makes substantially the same point when he asserts that equity requires 'discrimination by reference to morally relevant differences, and forbids discrimination in the absence of such differences'.[50] How far will this suggestion take us? There is this to be said in its favour, and it is a point of considerable importance. Without some conception of what is morally appropriate or relevant the conditional equality formula is a virtually empty requirement. Unless we indicate what differences are to count in the distribution of burdens and benefits among men almost any distribution would be covered by the formula; as Kelsen puts it, it is consistent with 'any privilege whatever'. Yet the idea of what is morally appropriate or morally relevant may serve to cover such a wide assortment of moral beliefs and principles that forms of discrimination condemned by, say, humane liberals can nevertheless get their blessing from it. Is there anything like a consensus among moral philosophers on the defining features of morality, and are these features themselves sufficiently precise, to rule out what to liberal humanitarians are unjustifiable inequalities? Moreover, what of those who, like Max Stirner or Nietzsche, are commonly taken to repudiate ordinary conceptions of morality?

Clearly there are difficulties about this suggestion and to consider it at all fully would be a major undertaking far beyond the scope of this book. But let us explore it a little further. Adapting some remarks made by Professor Phillips Griffiths the idea could be presented thus: for a reason to be acceptable as a justifying reason for differential treatment it must satisfy the conditions of moral discourse. According to Griffiths there are three ultimate principles which together define the necessary, but not sufficient, conditions of moral discourse. (At one point Griffiths says that these principles, 'factors of the most general moral relevance' as he calls them, must be assumed to be correct 'if moral discourse is to be possible at all'; yet elsewhere they are described as necessary for 'establishing any correct moral theories, rules, or particular judgements'.[51])

The three principles are: (i) impartiality; (ii) rational benevolence; and (iii) liberty. The principle of impartiality is the demand for universality, i.e. 'any action which it is right or wrong for one person to do is right or wrong for every person to do unless there are some special factors present in the other cases'. This formula looks to have much in common with the principle of conditional equality and indeed Griffiths goes on to add that the call for similar treatment in similar cases is a general form of the particular requirement of justice, i.e. 'any form of treatment which is thought to be right for one man must be right for all others, unless the others are significantly different'.

The second ultimate principle—rational benevolence—lays down the requirement that any proposed action should take into account the interests of all persons, 'the interests of all rational beings whatsoever'. Here again, the principle suggested bears a striking resemblance to what Carritt and others have called 'equality of consideration'. So it turns out that if we take these two principles as together constituting part of the necessary conditions of moral discourse, the principles of conditional equality and of equality of consideration are built into morality or at least into 'correct moral theories, rules, or particular judgements'.

Griffiths' third principle, liberty, specifies that we respect the right of every rational being to follow his chosen course of action, that 'special justification' is required before there can be interference with such an agent's freedom of choice. This principle may seem somewhat less relevant to equality and in view of the way the 'national interest', the 'common good' or the 'cause of progressive humanity' have been invoked by rulers to curb or stifle dissident opinions and activities (and such repression may be regarded as a particular kind of differential treatment) one could with good reason feel cynical about the effectiveness of this requirement, at least until the notion of 'special justification' had been elucidated. On the other hand, it puts the burden of proof on those seeking to restrict freedom and this is a common move in the argument for liberty; but it is only one move and obviously a good deal more would have to be added before we could say that a case had been made out. And it has to be said that Griffiths admits this. Indeed, of all three principles he explicitly warns that formidable problems of application in concrete situations must inevitably arise, not only in respect of each single principle but also in the relationship of each to the others. This of course is a characteristic problem in the application of general rules and principles—how are they to be interpreted, what counts as the correct way to follow them, how many alternative courses of action do they permit? It would be foolish to hold this difficulty against Griffiths unless one thought that his principles were unusually open-ended, for one might equally well argue that theft or freedom of the press were useless notions and carried no implications for action, which is absurd.

Let us take stock. We have been considering the suggestion that the conditional equality principle ought to be construed such as to yield more than just an empty formula by specifying that the reasons to be advanced for differential treatment must be 'morally relevant'. Now I think it has to be recognized that arguments about equality, in our society at least, do commonly take place between disputants who on both sides would regard their reasons, with some justice, as morally relevant. Whether or not to discriminate against those who take certain drugs, homosexuals, those with a low I.Q., coloured immigrants and so on are questions over which controversy largely goes on *within* the limits of moral discourse as conceived by Griffiths. It is at any rate not obvious to me that this is not so.

Even on an issue which has figured so prominently in arguments about equality over recent years—apartheid in South Africa—the defenders of discrimination contend that their policy is consistent with a belief in humane values. The more sophisticated exponents of the policy would certainly reject the charge that they abandon reasoned argument and would assert that the case they put up for their policy, unacceptable and abhorrent though that policy may be to others, is of a different order from the ravings of a Hitler or a Julius Streicher about the Jews. Thus we find them saying that they accept the liberal principle that each man is entitled to the fulfilment of his potentialities, and starting from this principle they go on to claim that the fact of being black makes a difference, since persons of that colour in their society require different conditions for their fulfilment. The creation of a series of Bantustans is said to cater for their cultural distinctiveness and constitutes the best framework for the realization of their capacities. And we should notice that this sort of argument has percolated down from the philosophers and theologians to the politicians. The South African Minister of Defence was reported as saying in December 1964: 'We must accept the basic principle held in the world that all people are entitled to equal opportunity. But there is a world of difference between equality and sameness.' He went on to urge that the differences between the population groups should be recognized and that the two main colour groups should be led to full sovereignty in their own areas.[52] Now we do not have to agree with the policy of apartheid to concede that its advocates (or at least some of them) attempt to make out a reasoned case which, prima facie at any rate, satisfies Flathman's conditions of 'giving reasons'. And, as we have noticed, they start out from what is virtually the principle of conditional equality; which reinforces the claim that the mere assertion of the conditional equality formula, without further ado, decides virtually nothing in the problems of allegedly unfair discrimination that concern us in the world today. If this can be said of the policy of apartheid, how much more could it be said about the controversies over such issues as the distribution of wealth and inequality of opportunity in education?

When the liberal humanitarian proclaims his opposition to apartheid his case against it cannot receive much help from the bare formula of conditional equality. He may wish to maintain, though, that the idea of taking the interests of all rational beings into consideration rules out racial discrimination of any form, including apartheid; and among the several counts in his indictment would be the fact that the South African Blacks have no real say in framing the policy which affects their interests so fundamentally. The requirement that the interests of all persons be equally considered is, as we have seen, taken by Griffiths to be one of the defining characteristics of moral discourse. For Carritt, too, it enters into what is a morally relevant reason for discrimination. But how powerful a weapon against unjustifiable discrimination is the injunction that the interests of all persons should be equally taken into 'consideration'?

The kind of force which some philosophers want to impart to 'consideration' is illustrated by Rashdall's assertion that every human being is of equal intrinsic value and hence equally entitled to respect; and for him this carries the implication that men are all possessed of certain basic rights. Or as Frankena puts it, the meaning of the equal intrinsic value of all persons is that we should be concerned for the good lives of every individual; the just society, he says, 'must, so far as possible, provide equally the conditions under which its members can by their own efforts (alone or in voluntary associations) achieve the best lives of which they are capable. This means that the society must at least maintain some minimum standard of living, education, and security for all its members'.[53]

If this is the intent behind the principle of equality of consideration the word 'consideration' has seemed to some writers a rather feeble way of expressing so important a moral idea. Raphael speaks for more than himself when he says that 'consideration' is too weak a term to perform this function.[54] When we say of a person that he should receive consideration or that his interests should be taken into consideration, is this to require anything more than simply that his claims ought not to be ignored? Clearly it cannot mean that all his claims and/or interests have to be accepted as legitimate and hence satisfied. Did the Jews receive 'consideration' from the Nazis? As Rashdall and Carritt want the term to be understood, certainly not. Equality of consideration, they propose, carries with it the commitment to respect the rights of all men, irrespective of race or religion and, it would be argued, this is just what the Nazis failed to do in their treatment of the Jews.

It is evident, however, that if general principles such as equality of consideration are to convey the full force that those who adopt them want them to have a good deal of elucidation is required. A recent example of the attempt to give substance to the notion is a paper by Stanley Benn in which he gives an account of what he understands by 'the equal consideration of human interests'.[55] We cannot follow the details of his argument here save to notice his warning that the principle 'can be effective in public policy-making only to the extent that agreement can be reached on the proper order of priority of human interests'.[56] Apart from the difficulty of reaching such an agreement in the first place—men notoriously disagree on whether, for example, freedom has the same degree of priority (assuming we have a common notion of what 'freedom' is) in the so-called under-developed countries or when the class enemy has to be overthrown—there is always the problem of specifying the circumstances in which a particular interest can be overridden by an appeal to the common good or the national interest. But what we want to say about the treatment of the Jews in Nazi Germany, for example, is that *no circumstances* could ever justify that. And in taking that sort of stand general declarations of human rights or schemes of priority of human interests are of little help. Because they are so general, because it is so widely granted that they allow of exceptions—'no human rights are absolutely unconditional'— they offer at most broad guidelines which the complexity and painful dilemmas of practical politics often render ambiguous and tentative. As Griffiths puts it: 'the problem of the application of these principles to particular situations . . . [is the one out of which] all the really important and difficult questions of substance in ethics arise'.[57]

I asked earlier if there would be a consensus among moral philosophers on the conditions or distinguishing features of moral discourse. Of course the very idea that an enquiry into the nature of moral discourse is necessary to demonstrate that the Nazi treatment of the Jews was monstrously evil is grotesque. But the forms of discrimination which mostly engage the attention of egalitarians are not of this order and if a limit is to be set to the reasons which can justifiably be advanced for differential treatment the suggestion that these reasons should be 'morally relevant' has to be taken further. Griffiths, we noticed, alternates between saying that his three ultimate principles are necessary conditions of moral discourse as such and, on the other hand, of *correct* moral judgements. I am not sure what significance should be read into this difference. Would it be fanciful to suppose that he can recognize the position of someone who rejected one or more of his principles as a 'moral' one but that it involved a different conception of morality from his own and that, in his view, an incorrect conception? If this is a legitimate interpretation of Griffiths' remarks it clearly adds to the difficulties of determining what is 'morally relevant'.

Quite apart from his, it has to be accepted as an unpleasant fact that there is no agreement as to what constitutes morality; on the contrary, much disagreement. Consider such an obvious example as the conflict between utilitarians and their critics, as well as the significantly different ways in which utilitarianism itself has been formulated. Or consider the criticism into which Professor Hare's notion of the universalizability of moral judgements has run—a notion which, incidentally, is very similar to Griffiths' principle of impartiality. And Philippa Foot's attempt to show that 'moral virtues must be connected with human good and harm, and that it is quite impossible to call anything you like good or harm', has also come under a good deal of heavy fire.[58] Moreover, the utilitarians, Hare, Foot and the bulk of their Anglo-American critics could be said to all belong within a moral tradition which a Max Stirner or a Nietzsche would repudiate. For these reasons, and the substance of them cannot be elaborated here, the suggestion that what is 'morally relevant' will serve to define the limits to what are justifiable reasons for discrimination holds little prospect of success.[59]

At this point an obvious objection could be made that we do not need to have a consensus or even a viable theory on the *philosophical* issue of the nature of moral discourse in order to agree about what is moral. Is there not in fact a good deal of common ground among the disputing philosophers, as well as among ordinary persons, as to what are moral virtues, moral actions? But is there? About drugs, gambling, divorce, abortion, suicide, animal sports—to mention but a few matters on which there is notorious disagreement? Let us turn to problems where the principle of equality is typically involved, and let us assume that all disputants would say that racial discrimination is an evil. Are they unanimous about recent British governmental measures to control the entry of coloured immigrants? Are they all so much in favour of educational equality as to support the abolition of the private sector in education? Do they all want to see a radical redistribution in the ownership of wealth? Do they all condemn discrimination against non-Marxists in Communist universities? And where do the theologians and philosophers of the Dutch Reformed Church fit in here? In the underdeveloped countries, do all morally conscientious persons demand that no one should receive more than the basic necessities of life until there is an end to malnutrition and other elementary deficiencies? How does the notion of 'moral relevance' help to decide between the satisfaction of basic needs on the one hand and the need for incentives and economic growth on the other? A number of philosophers have in fact taken the equal satisfaction of 'basic needs' to be the essential and fundamental requirement of equality and I myself sympathize very much with this view, though I have reservations about the ease with which, it seems to be claimed, we can draw up a commonly agreed list of these needs and arrive at an approved order of priority among them (how, for example, would we fix the relative weights to be attached to certain specified standards of housing and freedom of speech?). Now are we to say that someone who wishes to put more emphasis on incentives and economic growth (assuming that they are inconsistent with satisfying the basic needs of all men) is necessarily immoral? Countries at war have often to impose restrictions on the means of satisfying basic needs, so do developing countries which aim at rapid capital investment or have to maintain large armies. We may think such policies regrettable —but *immoral*? Well, if they are to be judged immoral, and this conception of morality is to be read into what are legitimate reasons for discrimination, so much less agreement will there be on any proposed principle of equality.

IV

Equality, Sir Isaiah Berlin has said, 'is one of the oldest and deepest elements in liberal thought'.[60] The sheer persistence of equality in the declared values of liberals and socialists seems to go against the difficulties we have encountered in the attempt to frame a viable principle of equality. Absolute equality is not seriously held by any liberal or socialist thinker, and the principle of conditional equality has shown itself to be too open-ended to convey the substance of what egalitarians are after.

Equality of consideration, or at least the elucidation it is commonly given, comes nearer to the heart of things, as does its allied notion of equality of satisfaction of basic human needs. The latter imply a moral attitude to one's fellow-men which for the religious person is partly expressed by saying that each person is precious in the eyes of God or, in a secular version, by a declaration of human rights. When people say that every human being is of equal moral worth they do not suppose that we are equally moral—equally honest, truthful or considerate— rather they mean that respect for each man's life, liberty, and security is an obligation on us all and that there is a duty on governments to realize these values by appropriate laws and institutions. Nor do they mean that, for instance, no man's liberty may ever be curtailed, but rather that a good and sufficient reason is always necessary for restricting men's freedom.

'Good and sufficient reason', we have seen, is a troublesome phrase, yet there are occasions when it has to be used. It indicates that the right to liberty is not absolute, though it fails to spell out the conditions for its use. To say, therefore, that all men are endowed, as men, with certain human rights and that in this respect they are all equal is clearly not to offer a detailed prescription for action; nor is it a guarantee against lip-service being paid to the idea by rulers whose conduct is blatantly at odds with its purpose. Moreover we have to insist again that the attempt to realize this idea in practical social policy and political action is beset with many difficulties, for some of the rights we specify can often give rise to conflicting demands and what they mean in a concrete situation is frequently in dispute. There are too many parts of the world where their immediate attainment is almost a utopian aspiration and even in the more liberal 'developed' countries there will be times when they will be subordinated to the needs of the nation's survival in periods of crisis. Hence in saying that men still have these rights when the effective exercise of them is impossible we are postulating a standard of achievement, offering a set of criteria in terms of which the performance of governments should be judged.

It is a moral perspective of this sort which goes with Rashdall's affirmation of the intrinsic value of every human being and Tawney's call for society to provide those conditions of life which men need for the development of their varying capacities. It is an assertion of human equality in the sense that it manifests an equal concern for the well-being of all men. On the one hand it involves a demand for the removal of those obstacles and impediments which stand in the way of the development of human capacities—that is, it is a call for the abolition of unjustifiable inequalities. On the other hand, the demand itself gets its sense and moral driving force from the recognition that 'the poorest he that is in England hath a life to live, as the greatest he'.[61]

8/Some Remarks on 'Justification'

Ultimate values, it is often said, cannot be justified. Justification involves an appeal to other considerations, to facts and other principles. Since no set of facts entails any moral conclusion and since, in the nature of the case, there are no higher principles than ultimate values there is nothing further to which to appeal. Equality is commonly regarded as just such an ultimate value and hence, so it is claimed, it cannot be justified. One can be either for or against it. Yet some of those who have stood for equality seem to have *argued* for it. Are all such arguments necessarily spurious, rhetoric designed only to persuade? Can no case be made out for equality in the way that Mill and Hayek have argued for liberty?

Bertrand Russell put forward one particular version of the view that ultimate values lie beyond what can be justified. As opposed to arguments in science, where evidence can be adduced, arguments about values, says Russell, cannot be backed by evidence. The parties to a dispute about values can only appeal to the emotions. Thus Bentham's doctrine that the interests of each person were to count for as much as those of any other person collides head-on with Nietzsche's belief that only great men are important on their own account. 'We have here,' Russell says, 'a sharp disagreement of great practical importance, but we have absolutely no means, of a scientific or intellectual kind, by which to persuade either party that the other is in the right.'[1] The only methods we can adopt to alter men's opinions on matters of this kind 'are all emotional' not intellectual'.[2] In a somewhat different vein Sir Isaiah Berlin too holds that there can be no question of justifying equality. He says: 'Belief in equality—fairness—the view that unless there is a reason for it, recognized as sufficient by some identifiable criterion, one man should not be preferred to another, is a deep-rooted principle in human thought . . . Like all human ends it cannot itself be defended or justified, for it is itself that which justifies other acts— means taken towards its realisation.'[3]

But there are a few voices on the other side and some of what they have said will be either incorporated in, or commented on, in this chapter. An essential preliminary, however, is to sort out the various elements which have gone to make up the idea of equality in order to see whether, and if so how, the question of justification can arise.

1   Our first candidate can be dismissed briefly. Absolute equality—treat all persons in the same way in all respects—does not recommend itself to anyone and so there is no call for its justification. On the contrary, precisely because its implementation (if that were possible) would violate our ordinary notions of justice and conflict with values such as individuality and freedom of choice our reasons for rejecting it may be said to be an important consideration in favour of a more flexible principle. In other words, to the extent that respect for individuality and the satisfaction of the varying needs of men go against absolute equality so they support a conception of equality which can accommodate them.

2   We come therefore once more to the principle of conditional equality—'no discrimination without a reason', to put it for the moment in its barest form. Some writers say that one should *give* reasons for differential treatment, without indicating whether any significance is to be attached to the word 'give'. But clearly one must *have* a reason before one can give it. We shall therefore at this stage concentrate on the claim that there must *be* a reason (or reasons) or that one should *have* a reason (or reasons) if discrimination is to be legitimate, without going into detail just here on what sorts of reasons they have to be.

It might be thought that there are really two distinct propositions contained in this minimum version of the conditional equality principle: first, that one must have reasons for differential treatment; and, secondly, that there is a presumption in favour of treating all persons equally. The point of stating these separately could be to spotlight the problem of justifying the initial assumption that all persons should be treated equally, that, in some sense, we take all human beings to be on the same level. As it is sometimes put, the requirement that there must be reasons for differential treatment rests on the assumption that 'equality needs no reasons, only inequality does so'.[4] Or, as Monroe Beardsley argues, the burden of proof rests on those who make a claim for unequal treatment: the claim for equal treatment, he contends, needs no defence; what requires a reason is the claim to an unequal share. It is Beardsley's view that the equality injunction, as he calls it, when put in the form of 'All persons are to be treated alike, except where circumstances require different treatment' is a 'metamoral axiom', i.e. 'a rule for adopting rules' as opposed to a substantive moral principle.[5] If the formula were to contain 'should be' or 'ought to be' instead of 'are to be' then, he suggests, it would be a moral principle and as such either provided with a justification or simply regarded as an ultimate value. But as it stands it specifies 'only a [logical] requirement to supply a good reason for treating people unequally'.[6] Now if it is true that there is a *logical* requirement to advance reasons for discrimination ('a *good* reason' bothers me here, but let that pass) this looks to be a significant first step in the case for conditional equality. Whether such a case can amount to a 'justification' is another matter, but it would certainly cast doubt on the claim that there is nothing of an 'intellectual' (in contrast to 'emotional') sort to be said for equality.[7]

I have been arguing that in the typical contexts where the question of differential treatment is raised those who discriminate do have reasons; that where discrimination is introduced or carried on as a matter of public policy, when it is a widely known social practice, as in the cases of measures directed against Jews, Blacks in the United States and South Africa, homosexuals, Catholics in Northern Ireland or dissenters in the Soviet Union, the injunction to have reasons for differential treatment is superfluous since the discriminators are already complying with it. The issue in these and similar cases is whether the reasons are good reasons. But the objection may be made that I have loaded the question in my favour by specifying as the typical context one in which it is indeed difficult to imagine the discriminators not having reasons and, further, reasons that to them are sufficient. Is this not an attempt to *define* differential treatment, or at least certain forms of it, in such a way that from the notion itself it necessarily follows that there must be reasons? If discrimination, the objection might continue, is the sort of thing you say it is, then to ask for a justification for the 'requirement' that there be reasons for differential treatment is indeed a queer request to make. To all this I plead guilty and add that the question is already loaded in my favour, for let us remember that at this stage we are not saying anything about the nature of the reasons. Moreover we have ruled out the idea that the requirement applies to things such as the choice of one's friends. It is true that we can speak of a person as 'discriminating' in the choice of his friends, but is the choice itself discrimination? The making of friends is not necessarily something for which one has a reason; there may *be* a reason for some people, and not others, being one's friends, but that is 'a reason' in a different sense.

I maintain then that differential treatment without a reason, when it is undertaken consciously and deliberately as a matter of public policy, is something difficult to conceive of. Once the connection between 'reasons' and 'discrimination' is made clear would one ask for a justification of the 'procedure' of having reasons for discrimination? Yet there may be point to the injunction, 'Do not discriminate without a reason!' A judge or a teacher may allow his sour moods to influence his verdict or his essay marking and this could lead to an unjustifiable discrimination that he himself would recognize, i.e. there was nothing that he would regard as 'a reason' for the discrepancy in his decisions. Or a series of uncoordinated pension laws may lead unwittingly to serious inequities in the payments received by different classes of war veterans. Once the anomalies have been pointed out those in authority are under an obligation, and are likely to feel it necessary, either to make the appropriate changes or to attempt to justify what to others appear to be unjustifiable cases of discrimination—and that would involve giving reasons. What would strike us as extremely odd, to put it mildly, would be the response that though war veterans of class A do not differ in any relevant respects from those in Class B they do nevertheless merit higher pensions; or, that student X's essay was not appreciably better than student Y's yet rated a 30 per cent higher mark.

One possible motive in asking for a justification of the bare conditional equality formula could be a desire to be shown why having reasons for a policy or a decision is better than deciding by caprice. And we have seen that the formula has been construed by some writers as having the function of 'Don't act capriciously!' Now I have been assuming all along that the sort of discrimination we are mainly concerned with does matter, that both the discriminator and his critics agree on its importance. Granted this, does it make sense to suggest that acting capriciously is just as good a way of making decisions as the process of deliberation? For to maintain that it is would imply that any decision is as good as another, that it does not matter how people are treated. So far as I know no version of the principle of equality has ever been challenged on these lines. It might be thought from the language used by some of the cruder racists that they do not think it matters how certain racial groups are treated. But is specifying a particular group as unworthy of civilized treatment an example of caprice? Is not this discrimination? When, say, Jews or West Indian immigrants are singled out, but not Welshmen or Irishmen, does not this commit the discriminator to say that it *does* matter how some groups are treated and therefore that 'caprice' has to be used with discrimination?

The contrast that has been drawn—and it is frequently met with—between having reasons for decisions and deciding by caprice could be questioned on the ground that the very idea of 'deciding by caprice' is incoherent. 'Deciding', it might be said, implies deliberation whereas caprice is manifested in spontaneous action, no weighing of alternatives, acting on impulse and so on. But the matter is somewhat more complex than this, e.g. 'I suddenly decided to go out for a drink—I just felt like it'. It may also be held that there can be reasons for capricious actions, but surely the sense of 'reasons' then would not be the same as in 'justifying reasons'. Sometimes behaviour is characterized as capricious when there is no consistency about it. If a magistrate were to be severe on red-haired persons some days, bearded youths on others and people wearing bow-ties on yet others we should say this was arbitrary and/or capricious. But there could be 'reasons' for his behaviour, 'explanatory reasons'. However, further refinements in analysis do not affect my contention that the purpose of the conditional equality formula is, in part, to enjoin us to approach problems of differential treatment in the spirit of careful deliberation rather than caprice, and on the assumption that it matters how people are treated this is an injunction with many considerations of an 'intellectual sort' on its side.

One occasionally meets the question, 'But why do I need to have a reason for differential treatment?' This is puzzling. Does the questioner intend to suggest that we should not have reasons for doing things, *any* things? How could we give up 'having reasons'? I do not mean the sorts of things in respect of which it would be wrong anyway to claim that we have reasons for 'doing' them—or at least 'reasons' in the relevant sense. Do we have reasons for falling in love? For using the future tense? I mean rather not having reasons for buying a particular house, recommending university X to a school-leaver, wanting to reform the prison system or opposing the construction of another London airport. Granted there are occasions when it would either be absurd or wrong to ask for a reason, the idea that we might never need to have, or ask for, a reason simply cannot strike roots. All the more so when discrimination in the realm of public policy is involved and a particular person or group has been selected for differential treatment. It is idle to pretend that the characteristics of that person or group do not constitute the reason for discrimination. The person is, say, a university teacher of extreme left-wing views or the leader of a troublesome religious minority; the group is, say, the Jews, coloured immigrants or homosexuals. What would be the sense in asking why one needs to have a reason for discriminating against them?

I have tried to make it clear that in assenting to the minimum version of the conditional equality principle one is not committed to accepting the general rule, 'Don't act capriciously!' For as I have already stressed, capricious conduct has its place. If I am playing roulette or backing horses why not bet on the name or number that I fancy? Maybe successful gambling depends on the use of a system, but perhaps I don't want to bother, it's just an occasional fling. Saying, however, that caprice is not objectionable in certain contexts implies that in other contexts it is. I shall not try to frame a general formula to specify the areas or types of conduct where we should object to capricious decisions. I suspect anyway that any formula which purported to be wide enough to cover all cases would not be helpful, but one condition at least we should be likely to insist on is that when differential treatment is introduced and/or maintained by public bodies or officials there is a strong prima facie case against being capricious. Yet, paradoxical though it may seem, it is in the area of public policy and administration that this condition is rarely violated. Those in authority, I have been saying to the point of boredom, already have their reasons and usually feel obliged to give them. Political argument turns largely on the adequacy of their reasons.

3   If persons in authority do normally have reasons for differential treatment it is important that their reasons should be publicly stated, hence the injunction, 'Reasons should be *given* for differential treatment'. The conditional equality formula is sometimes phrased so as to make this part of its requirements. A good deal of the ground relevant to supporting this injunction has already been covered. In so far as discrimination is proposed or upheld by persons holding public office the case for having their reasons made public would coincide to a large extent with the argument for the general accountability of rulers to their subjects and this would take us into the whole question of what can be said for responsible government, which I do not consider necessary to go over here. Ministers sometimes invoke 'the public interest' in justification of withholding their reasons (too often many would say) but this is to imply that unless 'national security' or some other similar consideration is at stake there *is* an obligation to give reasons for decisions.

How far we should wish to extend this principle is of course a complicated and disputed matter. When is a university teacher entitled to plead 'confidentiality'? This became an issue in Britain in recent years during the course of the student protest movement. Is a student entitled to know in detail the reasons why he failed an examination? Is the applicant for a teaching post entitled to know the reasons why the selection committee preferred someone else? Now if there is a case for withholding reasons on some occasions in this sphere, even more so can it be said of 'private life'. Indeed it has been contended that the conditional equality principle has no relevance here at all. Does one have to account for having invited A, B, C and D to a Christmas party and not X and Y? Is it anyone else's business that I support certain charities and not others? When however a publican or shopkeeper refuses to serve specific groups of people the appeal to a 'right of privacy' is clearly less sustainable. With these reservations, and admitting that there will always be many difficult borderline cases, I would maintain that the requirement to *give* reasons for differential treatment can be supported by cogent *intellectual* argument.

4   The oft-expressed uneasiness about the emptiness of the conditional equality principle springs largely from the absence of any restriction on what is to count as 'a reason' for differential treatment. I have said that for the most part there *are* reasons for discrimination and this, if true, would seem to render it rarely necessary to assert the the principle as an injunction. But the term 'reasons', we have noticed before, can be ambiguous; it may be used in a 'causal' or a 'justificatory' sense.[8] Some philosophers have required of the grounds for discrimination that they be 'morally relevant' and this shows that they are thinking of reasons in the justificatory sense; and even if other philosophers have avoided speaking of 'morally relevant' reasons the clear implication of what they say is that they are referring to reasons that 'justify' rather than 'explain'. But lest there be any doubt about the force of 'reasons' in the conditional equality formula let us specify: 'The reasons given for differential treatment must be *justifying* reasons.'

It seems hardly necessary to have to make this point and that it is one which can be supported by argument of an 'intellectual sort' must be equally obvious. The distinction between explanatory and justifying reasons is a fairly elementary one and in many cases it is clear-cut. But what is offered by way of an explanation of an action or a decision can often be at the same time a justification. A man caught speeding at 120 m.p.h. might admit that he had had a few whiskies and wanted to see how fast his new car would go, realizing full well that his explanation does not amount to a justification. On the other hand someone else going at the same speed might explain and justify his conduct with the information that he was a surgeon and had been suddenly called to an urgent operation. Similarly a psychologist might discover that A's discriminatory treatment of the Jews was attributable to certain experiences in early childhood without wanting in any way to condone or justify A's conduct. The reasons for A's anti-Semitism are *discovered*, while the reasons A gives for his wanting to persecute the Jews can be *rejected*.

This last example points to an ambiguity in the demand for justifying reasons. Are we to require that the reasons given for discrimination do not only go beyond explanation but also amount to a justification acceptable to us—and to whom among *us*? Or is it enough that they seem sufficient to the discriminator? If the former then we are asking not merely for justifying reasons as such but for reasons of a certain specific character; for while the simple distinction between explanation and justification is not a disputed matter, the attempt to lay down conditions for what we shall regard as a *proper* justification will inevitably generate controversy. I conclude therefore that the requirement that the reasons given for differential treatment are to be *justifying* reasons raised no problem at this stage, for this is what they invariably are. But if anyone should want it, a case for this requirement, involving an account of the difference between explanation and justification, could easily be made out. I am aware that no writer who would suggest that the possibility of justifying the principle of equality, or advancing an intellectual argument in its support, turns on this issue.

5 'The reasons to be given for differential treatment must be both relevant and sufficient.' Here we come to what many consider to be one of the crucial aspects of conditional equality. The injunction lays it down that the reasons advanced have not only to be justifying reasons but also both relevant to, and sufficient for, the discriminatory treatment in question. Once again, however, one cannot but be moved to ask: Is anyone likely to adduce reasons which he thinks are irrelevant and insufficient? If he thinks, as he obviously must, that his reasons are both relevant and sufficient and others take a different view, what then? In respect of any particular form of discriminatory treatment there is room for argument and each side can try to persuade the other to change its position; but disagreement may persist. Now since it is notoriously the case that men do differ over the criteria (or, at least,

many of them) to be applied to justify unequal treatment, those who wish to uphold a particular interpretation of conditional equality have to make it clear what criteria they favour and why. (I shall defer more detailed discussion of this problem until later.)

Meanwhile, with regard to the general requirement that reasons must be both relevant and sufficient, who would want to argue against it? To stick to the criterion of 'relevance' for the moment. Any such person would not, *ex hypothesi*, be arguing for or against the relevance of a specific reason (or type of reason) but against the very idea that criteria for discrimination need to be relevant at all. It is difficult to imagine what he could say. Equally, it is not easy to see what could be said *for* the requirement of relevance, since to disclaim it would be plainly absurd. But that does not mean that our acceptance of this condition is an 'emotional' one; indeed we should be justified in suspecting the intellectual capacity of anyone who wished to reject it. As I see it he would be committed to something like this: 'Discriminatory treatment of group X is justified for reason Y, but I fully admit that Y is both irrelevant to, and insufficient for, this kind of treatment.' To repeat, agreement on this requirement does nothing to settle what in relation to the conditional equality principle are relevant and sufficient grounds for differential treatment.

Aristotle assumed that his readers would share the view that success in an athletic contest was not of itself a relevant qualification for public office and we should agree, recognizing however that renown in sport *may* be a factor in swaying votes toward particular candidates in popular elections (has Prime Minister Edward Heath's widely publicized success as a yachtsman brought him any electoral advantage?). No one in our society is likely to doubt that the number of letters in a person's surname shows nothing about his guilt and innocence before a criminal court or his fitness to enter a university. Similarly, the colour of a man's hair is considered to be irrelevant to eligibility for the franchise. But in some countries the colour of a man's skin is thought to be relevant, just as in others is a person's sex. Confronted with claims of this sort it is certainly possible to put forward a reasoned case by way of rebuttal and I do not see what a request for justification of the need for relevant and sufficient reasons could mean—apart from the general requirement about relevance just discussed—other than to ask whether a case can be made out for adopting or rejecting certain criteria for differential treatment. In this sense I would claim that the call to 'justify', or support with reasoned argument, this aspect of the conditional equality principle is one that can be met. But, let me emphasize again, it is important to recognize that when we invoke the conditional equality formula as a move in a controversy about discrimination we shall have to do much more than just establish the credentials of the relatively modest requirement considered in this section.

6 We now face the most difficult task in our stage-by-stage examination of the various elements which go to make up the principle of conditional equality, namely, to indicate what sorts of reasons are acceptable as grounds for differential treatment and to consider whether a case can be made out in their favour. To tackle it thoroughly would need a book to itself, for it has ramifications which spread over large areas of moral and political philosophy. What can be said here must, therefore, be taken as only a tentative and sketchy outline of a few of the issues involved.

We have arrived at the position of saying it is not enough merely to require of the reasons advanced in support of discrimination that they be relevant and sufficient. We have to go on to specify what sorts of reasons we do accept as legitimate and to consider whether a case can be made out for them. To some extent the ground has already been covered, since the rejection of absolute equality derived in part from the recognition of men's varying needs and capacities and of the importance of appropriate provision for these needs and capacities, and conditional equality allows for this. Now if it is possible to build up a case of this kind then one of the major demands implied in the request for a justification of equality will have been met.

There are at least two lines of approach we could take in this endeavour, which may be termed the 'positive' and 'negative' approaches. On the positive side one could attempt to elaborate on the conception of the intrinsic value of every human being put forward by writers such as Rashdall and Carritt. It is a conception which, among other things, calls for impartial and sympathetic consideration to be given to the needs and interests of every person by those who have a responsibility for their well-being. The idea of respect for each human personality and the principle of equality of satisfaction of basic human needs are inseparably linked to such a conception, as indeed is the doctrine of human rights. I am not supposing that the question of what these 'basic needs' are is beyond dispute, far less that there is a universally agreed order of priority among them. Nor do I suppose that the notion of 'legitimate human interests' is free from conflicting interpretations. The U.N. Declaration of Human Rights adopted in 1948 sets out a fairly comprehensive list of what most writers would include among basic needs and interests, admittedly in language which allows diverse constructions to be put on them. But I would certainly repudiate the suggestion that we cannot offer reasoned argument in support of one rather than another way of understanding and applying the more general clauses of the declaration.

Obviously, to elucidate these notions and principles and make out a case for particular ways of interpreting them clearly amounts to a formidable task, but it is one which a number of writers have undertaken and they have done enough to show that the task is a feasible one.[9] I shall not attempt it here, nor do I think it necessary for the limited purpose I have set myself. Let us, however, as a sort of specimen of a larger project, consider very briefly one of the most often proclaimed right of man, a right which would have to enter in a fundamental way into any conception of human needs and interests and which is essential to the idea of the intrinsic value of every human being—the right to life.

A sceptic might say it is not at all obvious that there is a right to life or even that we set a value upon human life. He would cite the frequency of wars (international conflicts on a global scale, local wars and civil wars), the use of increasingly deadly weapons, the growing number of death-dealing automobiles, political assassinations, pollution of the environment and the consequent hazard to human life and so forth. These are just a few of the activities of man, he would say, which testify to his disregard for life. But apart from the fact that some wars are fought, and some assassinations carried out, for the sake of a better life (erroneous though the beliefs may be), there are at least as many examples which could be cited to suggest that we do set a value on human life: hospitals and health clinics; speed limits, safety belts and breathalyser tests; warnings against cigarette smoking; measures against pollution; laws and moral pressure against murder; safety devices against death by gas and electricity; helicopter rescue services, lifeguards on bathing beaches and mountain rescue teams—and a host of others it would be tedious to enumerate. What sense would there be in the provision of these services were there no regard for life? Moreover, they are services which are increasingly available to all men, irrespective of race, religion or I.Q.; and if there are ways to buy a superior service, it is a disputed privilege.

But, it will be said, this is to evade the issue. The real question is, 'Can one *justify* regard for life?' Well, I don't know about 'justify', but what would be the implication of denying the right to life? Without wanting to argue that the protection of life is always the highest duty—

'death before dishonour', 'better death than slavery', 'we must sacrifice our lives for the sake of our children' (why would it be a *sacrifice* if there were no regard for life?)—I do wish to reiterate that if there were no concern for life it would be difficult to make sense of a whole range of basic social norms and practices. Why grow food, attempt to prevent and cure disease; what sort of obligation would there be to avoid inflicting pain and injury if the taking of life did not matter? How much of morality would survive if murder was of no account? What force would there be, for example, to 'Thou shalt not steal' if there were no 'Thou shalt not kill'? There would certainly be no place for equality of consideration or equality of satisfaction of basic human needs, nor could such ideas be conceivable, if there were no value put on the protection of life. Now does all this amount to a case for the right to life? And I have made no direct appeal to the fact that men generally have a desire to live.

To assert the right to life does not mean, of course, that it is absolutely and unconditionally wrong ever to take life. To many people at least there is no inconsistency in proclaiming the right to life and recognizing the right to kill in self-defence or in the defence of others, or advocating abortion, birth control and euthanasia. Indeed the arguments in favour of the latter depend on the special circumstances, which, in the eyes of the advocates, justify departure from the general rule—its being a *general* rule carries the implication of possible exceptions. Were there no general regard for life there would be no sense in singling out abortion or euthanasia as justifiable exceptions.*

The reference to the arguments in favour of abortion or euthanasia is an appropriate moment to consider one or two aspects of the nature of these arguments, for there is a problem here which is highly relevant to the quest for a 'justification' of equality. The case for abortion of course commands nothing like universal assent and it would be absurd to maintain that 'rational persons' support one rather than the other side in the controversy. Would an advocate of abortion be entitled to say that the case for it had been 'proved'? Would that be the same as saying that its advocates had built up 'a formidable case'? It might be less misleading to put it in the latter form because of the associations of the word 'proof' with formal logic and natural science; and 'proof' of guilt in a court of law is not like establishing a case for a change in

---

* What might be called a 'selective regard for life'—i.e. that, say, the lives of Jews, Spartan helots or American Indians are or were of no importance—does in fact accept the right to life but endeavours to restrict the scope of its application.

social policy. If someone were to ask, 'Is abortion justifiable?' is he asking for 'proof' or for a cogent case to be made out on its behalf? He cannot demand of whatever case be advanced that it should be unanimously accepted before it qualifies as a 'justification', for that would be to impose a requirement which could never be satisfied in any sphere of argument. Whether or not a reasoned argument, or a case embodying 'intellectual considerations', can be put forward in support of a policy or a principle is independent of its capacity to secure unanimous approval. Proof in formal logic or science, sometimes mistakenly taken as models for justification in ethics and social policy, is also independent of its capacity to gain universal assent, though what makes it a proof derives from standards of evidence and validity which are generally accepted by practitioners in the field, and these standards are themselves related to more widely held ideas about validity and evidence. For if, as many philosophers have contended, there were no common agreement on such concepts and standards we should never be able to say that something was true, that an argument was valid or that a particular case was well supported by evidence.[10]

Now when I claim that a case can be made out for the criteria we should appeal to in the differential treatment of persons the sort of case I have in mind is not such as to be governed by the standards that obtain in formal logic or scientific reasoning. Nor does it have to be a case that must win the assent of all sane and rational beings.[11] Are those writers who maintain that equality cannot be justified, that it is an ultimate value which simply has to be accepted or rejected and in respect of which there can be no argument of an 'intellectual sort', clear about the standards of justification they have adopted and to which aspects of equality they are meant to apply? It is true that what is a justification or a strong case for some persons need not be so for others. And some cases are stronger than others. It may also be said that if all you require for 'establishing a case' is that an argument of some sort be put forward then it could turn out to be a pretty feeble affair. Fair enough; but the presentation of a case can fall short of both deductive and scientific proof and yet be much stronger than the mere uttering of words or emotional rhetoric. Deciding what is a strong case is no simple matter, yet I would claim that, in a perfectly legitimate sense, it is appropriate to talk of establishing a case for equality, along the lines sketchily outlined in this chapter. Wittgenstein has a remark in the *Zettel* (78e) which, when suitably modified, could be our watchword here: 'Sufficient evidence passes over into insufficient without a definite borderline.'[12]

Let us return to the right to life. I was saying that were there no such right it would be difficult to see the sense in many other important social norms. What would a society be like where there was no concern to protect life, no restrictions of a legal or moral nature on the taking of life? What bearing has this on equality? Well, granted the right to life, the question arises of what must go with it in order to sustain and effectively protect life. The conditional equality principle makes the assumption that if men do have these rights the burden of proof lies on those who would exclude certain groups of people from (i) the protection of life, presumably on the ground that 'some lives don't matter'; and (ii) the necessities of life—food, clothing, housing, medical care, and so forth. In saying that nutrition and medical attention, for example, are necessary for life nothing outlandish about the basic needs of man is being postulated, though the specification of certain other 'needs' could well generate controversy.

The concept of need is one of the traditional criteria for differential treatment. To move above the subsistence line, the needs of a scientist are clearly different from those of an artist or a mountaineer. To establish that differential treatment is legitimate in order to satisfy certain needs means that we have to show the relevance of the proposed treatment to the needs or that various sorts of needs call for appropriate forms of treatment; and in the case of the necessities of life, or the conditions necessary for scientific research and similar kinds of pursuits, a reasoned argument is obviously capable of being made out. The conditional equality principle requires of any would-be discriminator to show what it is about any person or group of persons that would justify their exclusion from these rights and the non-satisfaction of their needs. Whatever reasons are advanced to support discrimination are then open to scrutiny and considerations of an intellectual sort would certainly be involved. In face of what we have said in support of the right to life he would have to meet that case and, if he accepted it, show why some persons are to be treated as exceptions; and the same would apply to the necessities of life and to the needs of particular professions and activities.

I suggested that there were two ways of approaching the task of identifying the legitimate criteria for discrimination. That they will tend to merge has been brought out in the last paragraph. The second method, the 'negative' approach, would consist of the critical analysis of the reasons given to justify the main types of discrimination which egalitarians nowadays find objectionable, such as the persecution of Jews, apartheid, inequalities in education and the maldistribution of wealth. In the course of the enquiry a positive commitment to certain values would inevitably reveal itself and the traditional criteria for differential treatment—need, merit, and capacity—are likely to emerge as focal points in the analysis. The elucidation of these concepts and the arguments for interpreting their claims in this rather than that way are common features in the literature of equality and I do not propose to go over that ground here.[13]

It is sufficient for my purpose that the issues are susceptible of discussion in rational terms, which does not mean of course that rational persons are bound to end the discussion in agreement either on the force of the concepts themselves or on their relative importance. There is plainly a large overlap in the two methods of approach; the distinction between them rests mainly on how we embark on the task in the first instance. But what really matters here and what is crucial to my thesis is that they constitutute a rational method of argument in favour of certain criteria of discrimination and against certain others. For this is sufficient to rebut the claim that equality, or at least this aspect of conditional equality, is a value which we simply have either to accept or reject. This chapter has aimed at questioning that claim and its purpose can be expressed in the words of J. S. Mill who, in a different context, contended that 'the subject is within the cognisance of the rational faculty . . . [that] considerations may be presented capable of determining the intellect either to give or withhold its assent to the doctrine . . .'[14]

Notes
and
References

(Details of books and articles, if not supplied in these notes, will be found in the bibliography.)

1/Introductory

1   Bottomore, T. B., *Classes in Modern Society*, p. 11.
2   Buonarroti, *History of Babeuf's Conspiracy for Equality*, p. 316.
3   Engels, F., *Anti-Dühring*, p. 121.
4   Engels, F., 'On Authority', p. 520.
5   Plato, *Republic*, pp. 36–7.
6   Locke, J., *Second Treatise of Government*, chap. 11.
7   Rousseau, J. J., *Discourse on Inequality*, p. 101.
8   Wilson, J., *Equality*, p. 40. Wilson makes the distinction in terms of 'natural' and 'artificial' differences. See Part 1, chap. 2. Melvin Tumin in *Social Stratification* remarks: 'Since ancient times social philosophers have been deeply concerned with economic, social, and political inequalities. They have theorized about the naturalness, permanence, and inevitability of such inequalities and have also asked whether they were good for any social purpose. Today these are still leading questions of students of social stratification' (p. 1).
9   As I point out later, from the fact that a rule or practice is 'conventional' it does not follow that it can be changed simply by a decision to do so. The practice of raising one's hat to a female acquaintance has largely died out, but there was no decision about it in the way that the rules of rugby were recently altered to upgrade the try in relation to the penalty goal. *A fortiori*, the concepts basic to a particular mode of thought are not 'mere conventions' in the sense that we can alter them at will. See P. Winch, *Nature and Convention*.
10 Rousseau, op. cit., p. 102.
11 MacIntyre, A., *A Short History of Ethics*, p. 17.
12 Ibid., p. 18.
13 Is a rabbit's death natural if killed by a bird of prey, but unnatural if shot by a farmer or if it dies from pesticides?
14 Rousseau, op. cit., p. 138.
15 Wilson, op. cit., p. 40.
16 Ibid., p. 40. What Wilson says here could be confusing. If two objects have the same value (e.g. two £1 notes) or two persons have the same rights (e.g. joint owners of a house), the equality in question is derivable from legal rules. But equality of 'power', in the sense of influence, is not like that. To say that two men 'have an equal voice in the government of a country' may be a reference to the law governing the franchise or it may refer to their 'power'. The latter is not a simple consequence of legal rules, even though a man's influence may be exercised 'within' a given legal framework.

17 Wilson, op. cit., p. 40. See also W. T. Blackstone, 'On the Meaning and Justification of the Equality Principle'.

18 Ibid., Part I, chap. 2.

19 Of course, a man's *seeing* a cheetah do this makes it no less 'natural'!

20 There may, of course, be a natural right to property which the law does not recognize.

21 Note the way Hume regarded certain social norms as 'natural' even though they were the products of social experience. See *Hume. Theory of Politics*, edited by Frederick Watkins, p. xiv.

22 Plato, *Protagoras*, pp. 54–5.

23 *Hume. Theory of Politics* (ed. Watkins), p. 72.

24 Ibid., pp. 32–3. (See also Hume, *Inquiry*, p. 124.)

25 Ibid., pp. 38–9.

26 Hart, *Concept of Law*, pp. 186 ff.

27 Winch, P., *Nature and Convention*, p. 242.

28 An example of the nature/convention dichotomy in recent egalitarian literature can be found in *Twentieth Century Socialism* (Penguin Books, 1956): 'It is not the differences which nature has ordained or fate decreed, against which socialists have protested; that would be nonsense. Their revolt has been against the privileges which society concedes to some and not to others.' (p. 24).

2/Inequality of Wealth

1 Bottomore, op. cit., p. 11.

2 Buonarroti, op. cit., p. 12.

3 In *Tribune*, March 15, 1968, J. E. Miller writes: 'Perhaps, like the total abolition of social inequality, the complete elimination of vice is not attainable. But Socialists, at least, must always act in the belief that it is. It seems quite senseless, otherwise, to talk about either human dignity or full equality of the sexes.' Allowing for the fact that this extract appeared in a review of a book by Fernando Henriques on *Modern Sexuality* it still seems surprising that anyone should be able to conceive of 'the *total* abolition of social inequality'. It is not only that anyone should think this a worthy goal, though this would be baffling enough, but also that it should be thought even remotely possible, i.e. as 'perhaps . . . not attainable', for *human beings*. The language is extravagant probably because Miller has not tried to think out what would be involved in 'the total abolition of social inequality'. Contrast Miller's language with that in the declaration of socialist principles issued by the Socialist Union (*Twentieth Century Socialism*, Penguin Books, 1956): 'Equality does not mean uniformity . . . The very diversity of individual fulfilment is an enrichment of society, to be encouraged and cherished, not ironed out of existence.' (pp. 23–4).

4 On the relationship between power and wealth, see Tumin, *Social Stratification*, chap. 5.

5 Tawney, R. H., *Equality* (1938 edition), p. 61.

6 Ibid., p. 56.

7 Ibid., p. 28.

8 *Equality* (1964 edition), p. 16.

9 See also J. H. Westergaard, 'The Withering Away of Class', in *Towards Socialism*, edited by Anderson and Blackburn, 1965.

10 James Dickens in the *Sunday Times*, April 13, 1969. A Labour Party report issued in August 1969 remarked that 'Britain remains a society in which there are very sharp divisions of wealth and income'. The report quotes 'the latest official estimates' to the effect that nearly a third of total personal

wealth is owned by one per cent of all adults, and that the richest 10 per cent own 74 per cent. (*The Times*, August 21, 1969.)

11 Among other things, the alleged effect on savings and incentives, and the question of the importance of having a thriving private sector independent of state control in industry, insurance, and education both on account of freedom of choice and because of the opportunities for innovation.

12 Roy Jenkins, in a speech reported in the *Guardian*, September 22, 1969, claimed that redistributive taxation by itself could not make any real impact on the position of the lower-paid workers or finance any appreciable advance in the social services.

13 Galbraith, J. K., *The Affluent Society*, p. 76.

14 Ibid., pp. 87–8.

15 This is to overstate the significance of the protest of the young. The traditional left in Britain, at any rate, has had a long and continuing interest in the inequality of wealth. Reference has already been made to some of the more recent literature. I would draw special attention to the following: Roy Jenkins, 'Equality', in *New Fabian Essays* (ed. Crossman, 1952); C. A. R. Crosland, *The Future of Socialism* (London 1956); *Towards Equality* (Labour Party, London 1956); Douglas Jay, *Socialism in the New Society* (London 1962); and the introduction to Tawney's *Equality* (London 1964) by Richard M. Titmuss.

16 Labour Party statement, 1969, reported in *The Times*, August 21, 1969.

17 Despite the proliferation of different brands of Marxism the importance attached to the ownership of wealth is still one of the central features of Marxian theory.

18 Jenkins, Roy, 'Equality', p. 69.

19 Ibid., p. 72.

20 Ibid., pp. 74–5.

21 On the record of the Wilson government in redistributing wealth, see Anthony Crosland, *A Social Democratic Britain* (Fabian Society, 1971), and Peregrine Worthsthorne, *The Socialist Myth* (London 1971).

22 Perhaps the most notable recent statements of this point of view are to be found in Quintin Hogg, *The Case for Conservatism* (Penguin Books 1947) and F. A. Hayek, *The Constitution of Liberty* (London 1960).

3/Political Equality: I

1 Mayo, H. B., *An Introduction to Democratic Theory*, p. 70. Note that Mayo regards his 'working definition' as 'normative' as well as 'operational' see pp. 69–71.

2 Everyman edition, pp. 216 and 208.

3 Constituencies in the 1970 General Election varied from Billericay with 124,215 on the electoral register to Birmingham, Ladywood, with 18,884. See the *Guardian*, June 1, 1970, p. 13.

4 I have drawn heavily on Frank Stacey's *The Government of Modern Britain*, chap. 11, in this section.

5 Stacey, op. cit., p. 48.

6 *New York Times*, February, 23 1964.

7 *Representation*, edited by Pennock and Chapman. Much of the material in the last three paragraphs has been drawn from this volume.

4/Political Equality: II

1 Lenin, V. I., *State and Revolution*, chap. v, p. 148.

2 Ibid., chap. v, p. 152.

3   Lenin, V. I., *The Proletarian Revolution and the renegade Kautsky*, London 1941, p. 30.
4   Laski, H. J., *State in Theory and Practice*, p. 161.
5   Ibid., p. 175.
6   Laski, H. J., *Marx and Today*, Fabian Society, 1943, pp. 16–17.
7   Marx, K., Preface to *A Contribution to the Critique of Political Economy*.
8   *Black Dwarf*, London, March 28, 1969.
9   It would be said in reply, no doubt, that the bourgeoisie (or its 'representatives') make precisely this sort of assumption when, in effect, it lays down that only activity in accordance with the constitution (i.e. a bourgeois constitution) will be permitted.
10 See for example M. Tumin, *Social Stratification*, and R. Dahrendorf, 'On the Origin of Inequality among Men', in Béteille, *Social Inequality*.
11 Mill, J. S., *Logic*, Book VI, chap. X.
12 Note the remarks by R. P. Wolff, *The Poverty of Liberalism*, on the way that the prestige of 'orthodox science' has had the effect of denying 'easy access to media of communication' to dissenting doctrines such as astrology and clairvoyance. This may be true of the United States, but a glance at some of the popular Sunday newspapers in Britain suggests that astrology at least gets a fair crack of the whip, 'officially ridiculed' though it undoubtedly is. I agree with Wolff that a proposal to establish chairs of astrology would get little support from even 'the most dedicated liberal'. (pp. 16–17).
13 I do not wish to deny that the Race Relations Act may contribute to achieving greater quality of opportunity between the races. Coercion is sometimes necessary to extend freedom.
14 But for recent troubles in Northern Ireland one might have been inclined to say that the attitude of Catholics toward Protestants and vice versa in the sixteenth century, because of the different cultural context, was quite a different phenomenon from the cases mentioned here in the text.
15 As I hope I have made clear, I am not assuming that the beliefs and values of a society are a monolithic structure.

5/Is Political Equality Possible?

1   Burnham, J., *The Machiavellians*, p. 97.
2   Ibid., p. 97–8.
3   Michels, R., *Political Parties*, pp. 406–7.
4   On the 'universality' of inequality, see Tumin, *Social Stratification*.
5   Bottomore, T. B., *Elites and Society*, p. 131.
6   Lawrence and Wishart, London 1940. Some writers maintain that Marx and Engels did not speak with one voice on the question of the state. See for example Robert C. Tucker, *The Marxian Revolutionary Idea*, chap. III.
7   Engels, F., *Origin of the Family, Private Property and the State*, p. 194.
8   Ibid., p. 196.
9   Ibid., p. 198.
10 Engels, F., *Anti-Dühring*, pp. 308–9. The original German, 'die Leitung von Produktionsprozessen', is sometimes translated as 'the direction', at other times as 'the conduct of the processes of production'. 'Die Leitung' can mean 'management', 'control', 'guidance' or 'leading'. 'Direction' seems an appropriate translation in this context, as the text goes on to suggest.
11 Engels, F., 'On Authority', pp. 521-2.
12 Ibid., p. 522.
13 The idea of the 'true interests' of society is troublesome for a number of

reasons. What are 'the interests' of society? Are they to be determined by reference to the aims and desires of the members of society? Which members? Are 'true interests' independent of the actual aims and desires of members of society at any given time? If so, how would such an idea be related to the claim that law and morality are class phenomena? Who is to be the final arbiter of the 'true interests' of society? Is there any independent test for determining such interests apart from the pronouncements of those who are charged with watching over them?

14 Marx and Engels, *Basic Writings*, ed. Feuer, p. 70.
15 Tucker, *The Marxian Revolutionary Idea*, p. 56.
16 Marx, *Eighteenth Brumaire*, pp. 130–1.
17 My emphasis.
18 *Basic Writings* (ed. Feuer), p. 441.
19 Ibid., p. 167.
20 Ibid., p. 201.
21 Ibid., p. 201.
22 *Basic Writings* (ed. Feuer), p. 407. See also Engels' letter to Bebel, March 1875, in which (inter alia) he refers to the 'notion of socialist society as the realm of equality' as 'a superficial French idea … '*Correspondence*, p. 337.
23 See Marx, *Poverty of Philosophy*, p. 147; and Engels' letter to Bebel of March 1875 cited in note 22.
24 *Basic Writings* (ed. Feuer), p. 522.
25 See letter to Bebel (1875) cited in note 22. But see also, G. Della Volpe 'The Marxist Critique of Rousseau', *New Left Review*, No, 59, January-February 1970, pp. 101–9.
26 But see J. B. Sanderson, *An Interpretation of the Political Ideas of Marx and Engels*, chap. VI. It is important to note that Engels' article, 'On Authority' (1874) and a letter to Cuno (January 1872), in which he expressed similar ideas (*Basic Writings*, pp. 481–2), were both written during Marx's lifteime. See also Michael Evans, 'Marx Studies', in *Political Studies*, December 1970, pp. 528–35.
27 Tucker, R. C., *The Marxian Revolutionary Idea*, pp. 90–1. Note references to Tucker by Michael Evans (see note 26).
28 Ibid., chap. 3.
29 *Capital*, III, chap. XXIII.
30 Ibid.
31 See Kamenka, E., *Marxism and Ethics*, chap. V.
32 Marx and Engels, *The German Ideology*, p. 483; and *Basic Writings* (ed. Feuer), p. 70.
33 Kamenka, op. cit., pp. 48–9.
34 Ibid., p. 49.
35 Though the dictionary gives 'constraint', 'compulsion' and 'restraint' as alternatives to 'coercion', some writers seek to limit its meaning to the use of physical means to secure compliance, others to 'a high degree of restraint' or 'severe deprivations': see W. J. M. Mackenzie, *Politics and Social Science*, p. 260 and Dahl, R. A., *Modern Political Analysis* (2nd edn, 1970), pp. 32–3. It is also common to find 'liberty' defined as absence of 'coercion' or 'constraint'. In view of these variations in its use it becomes something of a problem to determine if and when social relations are free of 'coercion'.
36 But see note 35.

6/Equality and Elites

1 Dahl, R., *Modern Political Analysis*, p. 6.

2 Beattie, J., *Other Cultures*, pp. 139 and 141.
3 MacIver, R. M., *The Web of Government*, pp. 7 and 21.
4 Dahl, op. cit., p. 59.
5 Lasswell and Kaplan, *Power and Society*, p. 226.
6 Tawney, R. H., op. cit. (3rd edn, 1938), p. 39.
7 Ibid., pp. 62–3.
8 Ibid., pp. 61–2 (my italics).
9 Ibid., p. 62.
10 Lasswell and Kaplan, op. cit., p. 226.
11 Dahl, op. cit., pp. 37–8.
12 Meisel, J. H., *The Myth of the Ruling Class*, p. 184.
13 Michels, op. cit., pp. 422–5.
14 Ibid., pp. vi–viii.
15 Ibid., p. 14.
16 Ibid., pp. 399, 400, 402 and 408.
17 Ibid., p. 408.
18 Ibid., p. 421.
19 Ibid., p. 418.
20 Ibid., pp. 423–4.
21 See the article on Michels by Juan J. Linz in the *International Encyclopedia of the Social Sciences* (1968), Vol. 10.
22 Article on 'Democracy' by Giovanni Sartori in the *International Encyclopedia of the Social Sciences* (1968), Vol. 4, pp. 112–20.
23 Bachrach, P., *The Theory of Democratic Elitism*, p. 38.
24 Ibid., pp. 85–7.
25 Ibid., p. 92.
26 Bottomore, T. B., *Elites and Society*, p. 129.
27 Ibid., chap. VII, especially pp. 139–40. Bottomore does not favour *complete* public ownership of economic units.
28 Ibid., p. 140.
29 Ibid., pp. 133 and 141.
30 Ibid., pp. 115 and 133.
31 Ibid., p. 133.
32 Bachrach, op. cit., p. 1.

7/The Principle of Equality

1 1938 edition, pp. 24, 26 and 27.
2 Everyman edition (trans. Warrington), pp. 134–5. *Stasis*, says Warrington, 'denotes the formation of a group (or that group itself) for the accomplishment of some political end, whether by legal or illegal means'. (p. 133). Sir Ernest Barket also translates *stasis* as 'sedition': *The Politics of Aristotle* (Oxford 1946), p. 204.
3 *Ethics*, V, p. 111.
4 The distinction between numerical and proportional equality appears in Plato's *Laws*. See Penguin translation of *The Laws*, pp. 229–30; and Everyman translation, pp. 138–9.
5 *Politics*, pp. 80–1, 86–9, 133–5, 174–6, see also *Ethics*, Book V.
6 *Politics*, p. 86.
7 All translations I have consulted give 'complexion'. Height would, of course, be a relevant consideration for recruitment into the police force or certain contingents of the armed services.
8 *Politics*, pp. 86–7.
9 *Politics*, p. 87.
10 Kelsen, 'Aristotle's Doctrine of Justice', p. 54.

11   Ibid., p. 55.
12   Oppenheim, Felix, 'Equality', in *International Encyclopedia of the Social Sciences*, Vol. 5, pp. 102–7.
13   Berlin, Isaiah, 'Equality', p. 303.
14   Lucas, J. R., 'Against Equality', pp. 296–7.
15   Watkins, J. W. N., 'Liberalism and Equality', *Spectator*, December 28, 1956, p. 927.
16   Oppenheim, F., 'Egalitarianism as a Descriptive Concept', *American Philosophical Quarterly*, April 1970, p. 144. See also article on 'Equality' by Oppenheim in *International Encyclopedia of the Social Sciences*, p. 105.
17   Watkins, op. cit.
18   Ibid.
19   Buonarroti, op. cit., pp. 315–16. Another translation of this passage appears in *The Good Society*, edited by Arblaster and Lukes, pp. 78–9.
20   Sir Isaiah Berlin in 'Equality' remarks that 'extreme equality'—i.e. 'the maximum similarity of a body of all but indiscernible human beings'—has not been advocated by any serious political thinker. Nevertheless, he says, such an idea 'possesses the central importance of an ideal limit or idealized model at the heart of all egalitarian thought'. (p. 315).
21   Charvet, John, 'The Idea of Equality as a Substantive Principle of Society' *Political Studies*, March 1969, pp. 1–13.
22   Ibid., p. 5.
23   Ibid., p. 4. Point is given to Charvet's argument by the report of a speech by Dr C. B. Hindley in the *Observer*, April 7, 1971. Speaking at the annual conference of the British Psychological Society, Dr Hindley is reported to have claimed that children from professional or semi-professional homes have an I.Q. score 25 points above those from the homes of unskilled or semi-skilled workers by the time they reach school age. Among the factors cited were: 'variety of toys, books and educational experiences provided by the parents . . . the breadth of the mother's vocabulary . . .'
24   Ibid., p. 5.
25   Williams, B., in *Philosophy, Politics and Society*, edited by Peter Laslett and W. G. Runciman, Oxford 1962.
26   Ibid., p. 124.
27   Ibid. (see pp. 123–7).
28   Ibid., p. 128.
29   Ibid., pp. 128–9.
30   This is to overstate the matter. A case could be made out for 'genetic engineering' to eliminate certain defects, e.g. imbecility and physical deformities, without any commitment to producing a uniformity above a given level of mental and physical 'normality'. A big question for the future is, where we draw the line? See the report in the *Guardian* (March 3, 1971) on the work of Professor Henry Harris and his colleagues at Oxford.
31   Tawney, op. cit. (1938 edition), pp. 25, 27–8.
32   *Sunday Times* (London), July 19, 1970.
33   On the controversy over Hume's famous remarks see *The Is/Ought Question*, edited by W. D. Hudson, Macmillan, 1969.
34   See Berlin, 'Equality', op. cit., pp. 314–15.
35   McCloskey, H. J., 'Egalitarianism, Equality and Justice', in *Australasian Journal of Philosophy*, May 1966, p. 56.
36   Ibid., p. 58.
37   Rashdall, *The Theory of Good and Evil*, Vol. I, pp. 223–4.
38   Ibid., p. 147.
39   Ibid., pp. 186–227.

40 Carritt, *Ethical and Political Thinking*, pp. 99, 157 and 81.

41 Perelman, Ch., *The Idea of Justice*, pp. 15–16.

42 Bowie, Norman E., 'Equality and Distributive Justice', *Philosophy*, April 1970, p. 141.

43 Raphael, D. D., *Problems of Political Philosophy*, p. 179.

44 Rashdall, op. cit., Vol. I, p. 147. W. T. Blackstone in 'On the Meaning and Justification of the Equality Principle' offers what he calls a 'pragmatic justification' of the equalty principle which has some points of similarity with what is said here and in the next chapter (for the record, the essentials of my argument were contained in a paper read at the University of Oregon in Eugene in February, 1964). Blackstone distinguishes two forms of the principle of equality: (i) what is in effect the principle of conditional equality, i.e. there must be relevant and sufficient reasons for differential treatment; and (ii) a 'context-dependent' use, in which certain criteria of relevance are specified, such as 'need', 'merit', 'capacity', etc. He says, quite rightly I think, that the request for justification has different implications in these two cases. But when he turns to elaborating his 'pragmatic justification' (pp. 250–51) it seems to me that he tends to forget this cautionary precept or, at least, to interpret it in an odd way. Drawing on Hart's paper ('Are there any Natural Rights?'), he says: 'If you want to have a system of morality in which the concept of "rights" is used, then you must adopt the equality principle . . . Hart's argument forces those who are committed to a certain view of society . . . to see that they can give up that principle only at a very high cost.' (p. 250). It is the manner of expression that I find so odd. 'If you *want* to have', and 'giving up', albeit at 'a very high cost'. What sort of price would one be paying? Applied to the first version of the equality principle these are indeed very peculiar things to say; as though we could 'want' to do without the practice of having reasons for discrimination, I mean *generally*. For it would certainly not be wanting to give up liberty for the sake of equality or wanting to join the Common Market. Similarly, could we want to do without criteria such as 'need' or 'merit', as opposed to the particular blend and weighting of them manifested in a given society or range of social policy, or in a person's moral outlook? Putting more emphasis on 'need' rather than 'merit', or vice versa, would make sense in a way that deciding generally not to have reasons for discrimination would not. I find it difficult to imagine anyone even trying to do this consistently; as, in a similar sort of way, it is difficult to imagine anyone embarking on a consistent policy of ignoring all evidence when making factual statements.

45 Flathman, R., *The Public Interest*, pp. 75–6.

46 Ibid., p. 76.

47 Let me repeat that Flathman's context is not ours; but I do not think this affects the point of my argument.

48 See *Annapurna South Face* by Chris Bonnington (London 1971), especially chap. I. The experience of the international team that set out to ascend the south-west face of Everest in 1971 is an unfortunate confirmation of this point.

49 Carritt, op. cit., p. 81.

50 Raphael, op. cit., p. 173.

51 Griffiths, A. P., 'Ultimate Moral Principles: Their Justification', in *Encyclopedia of Philosophy*, ed. Paul Edwards.

52 *The Times*, London, December 17, 1964.

53 Frankena, W. K., 'The Concept of Social Justice', p. 21.

54 Raphael, op. cit., pp. 186–7.

55 Benn, S., 'Egalitarianism and the Equal Consideration of Interests'.
56 Ibid., p. 62.
57 Griffiths, op. cit.
58 Foot, P., 'Moral Beliefs', in *Theories of Ethics*, p. 92.
59 On the question of what constitutes 'morality' see: Kurt Baier, *The Moral Point of View* (New York 1958 and 1965); W. K. Frankena, 'Recent Conceptions of Morality', in *Morality and the Language of Conduct*, edited by Castaneda and Nakhnikian (Detroit 1963); G. Wallace and A. D. M. Walker (editors), *The Definition of Morality* (London 1970); D. Z. Phillips and H. O. Mounce, *Moral Practices* (London 1970); and Peter Winch. *Moral Integrity* (Oxford 1968).
60 Berlin, op. cit., p. 326.
61 *Puritanism and Liberty* (ed. A. S. P. Woodhouse), London 1938, p. 53. Colonel Rainborough in the Putney Debates, 1647.

8/Some Remarks on 'Justification'

1   Russell, B., *Religion and Science*, p. 230.
2   Ibid., p. 230. See also pp. 235–43.
3   Berlin, op. cit., pp. 325–6.
4   Ibid., p. 305.
5   Beardsley, M., 'Equality and Obedience to Law', p. 36.
6   Ibid., pp. 36–7.
7   See the comments on Beardsley's paper in Blackstone, 'On the Meaning and Justification of the Equality Principle', pp. 240 and 253. But Blackstone's 'justification' of the principle of conditional equality is nearer to Beardsley's position than he seems to realize.
8   I am not assuming that 'reasons' are necessarily 'causes'. It is not necessary to my argument that I take sides in the controversy over the question whether the 'reasons' for human actions can be construed to be 'causes'. See Alan R. White (ed.), *The Philosophy of Action* (Oxford University Press, 1968).
9   See, for example, Hart, 'Are there any Natural Rights?' and chapters VIII and IX in the *Concept of Law*; Ginsberg, *On Justice in Society*; the papers by Frankena and Vlastos in Brandt (ed.), *Social Justice*; and the papers in *Political Theory and the Rights of Man*, edited by D. D. Raphael.
10 See, for example, Stephen Toulmin, *The Uses of Argument*, Cambridge, 1964; and Perelman, *The Idea of Justice and the Problem of Argument*.
11 Thus Frankena in 'The Concept of Social Justice': '. . . when we say that something in society is just or unjust we are purporting to judge it from a point of view which is fully free, informed, and rational, transcends both ourselves and our actual society, and is committed to a respect for the good life of every individual. And we are in some sense implying that every one else who so judges will eventually agree with us.' (pp. 26–7).
12 Wittgenstein, Ludwig, *Zettel*, edited by Anscombe and von Wright, Oxford 1967, S.439.
13 See, for example, the following: Frankena, 'The Concept of Social Justice'; Raphael, *Problems of Political Philosophy*, chap. VII; Blackstone, 'On the Meaning and Justification of the Equality Principle'; Feinberg, 'Justice and Personal Desert'; and Perelman, op. cit., especially chap. I.
14 Mill, J. S., *Utilitarianism*, p. 4.

Bibliography

ARBLASTER, A. and LUKES, S. (eds), *The Good Society*, Methuen, London 1971.
ARISTOTLE, *The Nicomachean Ethics of Aristotle* (edited and translated by Ross) Oxford University Press (World's Classics), London 1954 (1961 reprint).
—— *Politics* (trans. Warrington), Everyman's Library, London 1959.
BACHRACH, PETER, *The Theory of Democratic Elitism*, Little, Brown and Co., Boston, Mass. 1967.
BARKER, ERNEST, *Principles of Social and Political Theory*, Clarendon Press, Oxford 1951.
BEARDSLEY, M. C., 'Equality and Obedience to Law', in *Law and Philosophy*, edited by Sidney Hook, New York University Press, New York 1964.
BENN, S. I., 'Egalitarianism and the Equal Consideration of Interests', in *Equality*, edited by Pennock and Chapman (*NOMOS* IX).
BERLIN, ISAIAH, 'Equality', *Proceedings of the Aristotelian Society*, 1955/1956, pp.301–26.
BÉTEILLE, ANDRÉ (ed.), *Social Inequality*, Penguin Books, Harmondsworth, Middlesex 1969.
BLACKSTONE, W. T., 'On the Meaning and Justification of the Equality Principle', *Ethics*, Vol. 77, July 1967, pp. 239–53.
BOTTOMORE, T. B., *Classes in Modern Society* (2nd edn), Allen and Unwin, London 1967.
—— *Elites and Society*, Penguin Books, Harmondsworth, Middlesex 1966.
BOWIE, NORMAN E., 'Equality and Distributive Justice', *Philosophy*, April 1970, pp. 140–8.
BRANDT, R. B. (ed.), *Social Justice*, Prentice-Hall, Englewood Cliffs, New Jersey 1962.
BUONARROTI, P., *Buonarroti's History of Babeuf's Conspiracy for Equality* (translated from the French by Bronterre O'Brien), London 1836.
BURNHAM, JAMES, *The Machiavellians*, Putnam, London 1943.
CARRITT, E. F., *Ethical and Political Thinking*, Clarendon Press, Oxford 1947.
CHARVET, JOHN, 'The Idea of Equality as a Substantive Principle of Society', *Political Studies*, Vol. XVII, March 1969, pp. 1–13.
CROSLAND, C. A. R., *The Future of Socialism*, Jonathan Cape, London 1956.
DAHL, ROBERT A., *Modern Political Analysis* (2nd edn), Prentice-Hall, Englewood Cliffs, New Jersey 1970.
ENGELS, F., *Herr Eugen Dühring's Revolution in Science*, Lawrence and Wishart, London 1943.
—— 'On Authority', in *Marx and Engels. Basic Writings on Politics and Philosophy*, ed. Feuer.
—— *The Origin of the Family, Private Property and the State*, Lawrence and Wishart, London 1940.
FEINBERG, JOEL, 'Justice and Personal Desert', in *Justice* (*Nomos* VI), edited by Carl Friedrich and J. W. Chapman, Atherton Press, New York 1963.
FLATHMAN, RICHARD E., *The Public Interest*, John Wiley, New York 1966.

FOOT, PHILIPPA, 'Moral Beliefs', in *Theories of Ethics*, ed. Foot, Oxford University Press, London 1967.

FRANKENA, WILLIAM K., 'The Concept of Social Justice', in Brandt (ed.). *Social Justice*.

GALBRAITH, J. K., *The Affluent Society*, Penguin Books, Harmondsworth, Middlesex 1962.

GINSBERG, MORRIS, *On Justice in Society*, Penguin Books, Harmondsworth, Middlesex 1965.

GRIFFITHS, A. PHILLIPS, 'Ultimate Moral Principles: Their Justification', in *Encyclopedia of Philosophy* (ed.) Paul Edwards, Macmillan and Free Press, New York 1967, Vol. 8, pp. 177–82.

HART, H. L. A., 'Are there any Natural Rights?' in *Political Philosophy*, edited by Anthony Quinton, Oxford University Press, London 1967.

—— *The Concept of Law*, Clarendon Press, Oxford 1961.

HUME, DAVID, *An Inquiry Concerning the Principles of Morals*, edited by C. W. Hendel, Library of Liberal Arts, Bobbs-Merrill, New York 1957.

—— *Hume. Theory of Politics*, edited by F. Watkins, Nelson, Edinburgh 1951.

JENKINS, ROY, 'Equality', in *New Fabian Essays*, edited by R. H. S. Crossman, Turnstile Press, London 1952.

KAMENKA, E., *Marxism and Ethics*, Macmillan, London 1969.

KELSEN, HANS, 'Aristotle's Doctrine of Justice', in *Essays in the History of Political Thought*, edited by Isaac Kramnick, Prentice-Hall, Englewood Cliffs, New Jersey 1969.

LASKI, H. J., *The State in Theory and Practice*, Allen and Unwin, London 1935 (3rd imp., 1941).

LASSWELL, HAROLD and KAPLAN, ABRAHAM, *Power and Society*, Yale University Press, New Haven, Conn. 1950.

LENIN, V. I., *The State and Revolution*, Foreign Languages Publishing House, Moscow, n.d.

LUCAS, J. R., 'Against Equality', *Philosophy*, October 1965. Reprinted in *Justice and Equality*, edited by Hugo Bedau, Prentice-Hall, Englewood Cliffs, New Jersey 1971.

MACIVER, R. M., *The Web of Government*, Macmillan, New York 1947.

MARX, KARL, *Contribution to the Critique of Political Economy*—Preface, reprinted in *Basic Writings* (ed.) Feuer.

—— *The Eighteenth Brumaire of Louis Bonaparte* (trans. by Eden and Ceder Paul), Allen and Unwin, London 1926.

—— *The Poverty of Philosophy*, Martin Lawrence, London, n.d.

MARX, KARL and ENGELS, F., *Basic Writings on Politics and Philosophy*, edited by Lewis Feuer, Collins-Fontana, London 1969.

—— *The German Ideology*, Lawrence and Wishart, London 1965.

—— *Selected Correspondence*, Lawrence and Wishart, London 1934 (1941 reprint).

MAYO, HENRY B., *An Introduction to Democratic Theory*, Oxford University Press, New York 1960.

McCLOSKEY, H. J., 'Egalitarianism, Equality and Justice', *Australasian Journal of Philosophy*, May 1966.

MEISEL, JAMES H., *The Myth of the Ruling Class*, University of Michigan Press, Ann Arbor 1962.

MICHELS, ROBERT, *Political Parties* (trans. from the Italian by Eden and Cedar Paul), Jarrold, London 1915.

MILIBAND, RALPH, *The State in Capitalist Society*, Weidenfeld and Nicholson, London 1969.

MILL, J. S., *Considerations on Representative Government*, Everyman's Library, London 1957.
——— *Utilitarianism*, Everyman's Library, London 1957.
OPPENHEIM, FELIX E., 'Egalitarianism as a Descriptive Concept', in *American Philosophical Quarterly*, Vol. 7, April 1970, pp. 143–52.
——— 'Equality', *International Encyclopedia of the Social Sciences*, Vol. 5, pp. 102–7.
PARRY, GERAINT, *Political Elites*, Allen and Unwin, London 1969.
PENNOCK, J. R. and CHAPMAN, J. W. (eds), *Equality* (*Nomos* IX), Atherton Press, New York 1967.
——— *Representation* (*Nomos* X), Atherton Press, New York 1968.
PERELMAN, CH., *The Idea of Justice and the Problem of Argument*, Routledge and Kegan Paul, London 1963.
PLATO, *Protagoras and Meno* (trans. Guthrie), Penguin Books, Harmondsworth, Middlesex 1956.
——— *Republic* (trans. Lindsay), Everyman's Library, London 1948.
RAPHAEL, D. D. (ed.), *Political Theory and the Rights of Man*, Macmillan, London 1967.
RAPHAEL, D. D., *Problems of Political Philosophy*, Pall Mall Press, London 1970.
RASHDALL, HASTINGS, *The Theory of Good and Evil*, Oxford University Press, London 1907 (1948 reprint).
ROUSSEAU, JEAN-JACQUES, *The First and Second Discourses*, edited by R. D. Masters, St Martin's Press, New York 1964.
RUSSELL, BERTRAND, *Religion and Science*, Thornton Butterworth, London 1935.
SILLS, DAVID L. (ed.), *International Encyclopedia of the Social Sciences*, The Macmillan Co. and the Free Press, New York 1968.
STACEY, FRANK, *The Government of Modern Britain*, Clarendon Press, Oxford 1968.
TAWNEY, R. H., *Equality* (3rd edn), Allen and Unwin, London 1938.
——— *Equality* (with a new introduction by Richard M. Titmuss), Unwin Books, London 1964.
TUCKER, ROBERT C., *The Marxian Revolutionary Idea*, Allen and Unwin, London 1970.
TUMIN, MELVIN M., *Social Stratification*, Prentice-Hall, Englewood Cliffs, New Jersey 1967.
WILLIAMS, BERNARD, 'The Idea of Equality', in *Philosophy, Politics and Society*, edited by Peter Laslett and W. G. Runciman, Basil Blackwell, Oxford 1962.
WILSON, JOHN, *Equality*, Hutchinson, London 1966.
WINCH, PETER, 'Nature and Convention', *Proceedings of the Aristotelian Society*, 1959–60, pp. 231–52.

Index